I MIGHT REGRET THIS

ALSO BY ABBI JACOBSON

Carry This Book

Color This Book: New York City

Color This Book: San Francisco

I MIGHT REGRET THIS

*Essays, Drawings, Vulnerabilities, and
Other Stuff*

ABBI JACOBSON

virago

VIRAGO

First published in the United States in 2018 by Hachette Book Group
First published in Great Britain in 2018 by Virago Press

1 3 5 7 9 10 8 6 4 2

A CIP catalogue record for this book
is available from the British Library.

Hardback ISBN 978-0-349-01086-1
Trade paperback ISBN 978-0-349-01087-8

Book design by Marie Mundaca
Printed and bound by CPI Group (UK) Ltd, Croydon, CR0 4YY

Papers used by Virago are from well-managed forests
and other responsible sources.

Virago Press
An imprint of
Little, Brown Book Group
Carmelite House
50 Victoria Embankment
London EC4Y 0DZ

An Hachette UK Company
www.hachette.co.uk

www.virago.co.uk

DEDICATION TK

WHAT'S THE WORST THAT COULD HAPPEN

Before I make a decision, I tend to think about all the possible outcomes, the ways in which things could go down. I like to be prepared. This tendency unfortunately mainly includes obsessing over the ways in which things could go terribly off course, but it's better to be informed. So, before embarking on a solo cross-country drive that I would then write about in a book, I decided to make a list of possible worst-case scenarios. The road trip alone was terrifying, but writing about it afterwards? A lot could go wrong. So, what's the worst that could happen?

Heinous scenarios in which I'm hurt or die that I won't go into.

I adapt to eating only fast food while on the road and become someone who advocates for this new lifestyle. My politics change. I attend rallies for meat farms and even faster food. I go around encouraging people to stop caring, we're all going to die anyways!

I become a car fanatic. I learn the lingo, up my horsepower, and create an Instagram account just for my cars. I become the young Jay Leno.

After having not spoken to anyone for three weeks, I lose my voice completely. I have to find a voice double to dub in my voice on every acting project, and one day, while on the subway home from work, I break down because I realize I'll never become the singer I always dreamed.

I don't make it to Los Angeles. I take a wrong turn and end up in a small town somewhere in the middle of New Mexico. My car runs out of gas, so I have to stay the night in the local motel. While wandering around town the next day, I stumble upon a little shack and see a "For Sale" sign out front. I buy it and decide that this is my new life. I meet a lady bartender when I go to her bar alone and play The The on the jukebox. She likes that band too and we spend the night together. She moves in almost immediately. *Typical.* I start to carve wood after seeing a local artisan carving wood in his garage and I become his apprentice. I've always wanted to try carving wood. We start the New Mexican chapter of the Competitive Dual Wood Carving Association (CDWCA for short) and beat anyone within a hundred-mile radius in the Annual Southwestern Carvers Competition (ASCC). Also, is dual wood carving a thing? Shouldn't it be? I die next to my bartender, content, in our bed that I carved myself.

I get picked apart because driving across the country isn't the best thing for the environment. Or because my almond consumption is exhausting water supplies, or anything else I've done or written about in this collection that is bad for the earth. I know. I know, *I know*. I'm a shit and I'm sorry. But what about the fact that half the country eats a fucking cheeseburger 2x a week? What about that undeniable imprint and impact on the climate? We're all monsters, including me and my almonds.

Everyone will be like, *learn to draw hands already*!

People read the book and think, "What is this crap? A privileged white woman writes about how she's sad on her three-week vacation? Not for me." I *am* those things, and I did exactly that. I'm in no way denying how completely insane it is that I get to take off work for three weeks and drive around the country and then write about it…as more work. My life is bizarre and confusing to me as well.

Even though the book will be copyedited and proofread, my terrible grammar and lack of sophisticated vocabulary will shine through.

No one buys the book! If no one buys the book, the publisher could make *me* buy all the copies and I'll have to fill my apartment with books. I guess I could create furniture out of the books, piling them up like a sofa. I could throw pillows on top. I've had some time to think about this, and I could really make it work. Maybe my home, with its furniture completely built from my failed, unbought books, would make it into *Architectural Digest*? They'd come and take pictures and run a whole article about it. Who knows what could happen then!?

I'll get called out for not listening to the right albums, for playing the wrong podcasts, for not queuing up the most perfect playlist for the entire trip....I did my best.

All the pages somehow get numbered incorrectly!

I write about what it was like for me to fall in love with a woman and how I was clobbered when it ended and then I get banished from Hollywood! I'll never be the starlet I've always dreamed of, falling in love with Prince Charming on screen. FUCK THAT BULLSHIT. I can fall in love with Prince Charming or Princess Charming because Hollywood is changing. Anyone who only wants to watch the standard narrative better start collecting VHS tapes, because we're changing things. I want to be a part of telling real, more diverse love stories, ones I haven't seen on screen before.

That ultimately I'm admitting that I'm scared of being alone, and that will be seen as inherently pathetic. But aren't we all? Isn't that...the main thing? Aren't we all secretly terrified that we're not understood, not seen, not loved, not wanted? Okay, great, cleared that up.

A LOVE LETTER

In February of 2013, I received a love letter from 1944.

I had been out in Los Angeles for a few weeks, compiling the writers' room for *Broad City* and gearing up to start Season 1. I sublet my apartment in Greenwich Village to a friend of a friend while I was away, a sweet guy who watered my plant (hard *T*) and collected my mail. When I returned, I trudged up the stairs of my third-story walk-up with my luggage to find a large, neatly stacked pile on the kitchen counter. I'd never seen a few weeks' worth of mail at once, and immediately got excited—I *love* mail, and with a stack like this, the chances of me getting something good were higher. I'm talking *real* mail—a handwritten note or postcard from a friend, a small care package from my mom or dad or grandparent.

Real mail leaves an impression because it's an event—the surprise of receiving it, the examining of the envelope, and the reveal when you open it. It's tactile and ritualistic. When I was about seven, my grandparents accidentally sent my brother and me a postcard from their trip to London with two punks in leather jackets holding up their middle fingers straight to camera—we teased them about it for years. My other grand-father was a sort of mail connoisseur—he wrote me letters all throughout college; sometimes the letter would be covered in stickers, sometimes there'd be cash slipped inside, and other times there'd be a magnet his bank gave him for free. When I was away at overnight camp each summer, he'd send me care packages with fake cardboard bottoms he fashioned himself—he owned an Army and Navy Store, so he was often "fashioning things himself". There was always a letter included in the pack-age, resting on top of the boring packs of sports socks or Hanes T-shirts (to throw the counselors off), with instructions on how to pry open the perfectly fitted piece of cardboard he'd cut with an X-Acto knife. Underneath the fake bottom was neatly arranged candy and prank toys for my entire bunk. I loved finding that hidden loot. But it almost didn't matter what was inside the package, the act of receiving that loving gesture, directly from him to me, was enough. Now sending or receiving real, handwritten correspondence is like owning a classic car; it feels more thoughtful, curated, something you just want to run your hands along, but ultimately, it's no longer the most effi-cient way to drive.

Even owning stamps seems bizarre these days. Imagine go-ing to grab brunch with friends and someone says, "Hold up a sec, I have to pop into the bodega and grab some stamps." Everyone would be like: "For what?" "Bodegas have stamps?" "Also, what are stamps?" I don't think you'd even make it to brunch if they stopped to drop the letter in a mailbox. "You can use those blue things on the sidewalk!?" "I thought those were Banksys!?" We order more shit online than ever before and constantly get packages sent to us directly from the huge conglomerates taking over the world, but the thought of corresponding via snail mail with the people closest to us is absurd. What is happening to us?

The efficiency and speed of email and texting is something I obviously take part in and use, almost constantly, but the connection between us feels altered now. Like we never have to give more than part of ourselves when talking to anyone in *any* situation. We abbreviate, we rush delivery, we unsubscribe, we edit ourselves. When I was in college and communicating through social media was starting to really take off, for the first time, you could connect immediately with everyone you've ever met and anyone you haven't yet with one drunken click. Yearning for something more substantial, I did a project where I sent handwritten letters to twenty strangers in twenty different cities all over the country, to test what would happen. I found them randomly in the white pages, and shared something personal with each of them, a story about myself that was in some way associated with where they lived. I included another envelope (stamped already) with my address and asked them to write back sharing something of themselves with me. Would a connection be made? Would they, too, appreciate the long-lost art of letter-writing? Would this be the beginning of lifelong friendships and paper cuts (from opening so many envelopes)!? No, it wouldn't. *One* person wrote back. A teacher and soap maker who had gone to art school and appreciated my curiosity. I'd written her about my experience at a restaurant in the

Bay Area called Burma Superstar, and how my dad and I didn't order, but rather let the waiter bring out whatever he thought was best. I told her about how I'd never done that before and how it was one of the most delicious meals of my entire life. She sent me back a short, sweet note about the birth of her two children and how those days were her most memorable, her most remarkable. And that she too loved Burma Superstar. The experiment didn't go exactly as I'd hoped, but that one letter was enough for me. A small, meaningful connection with a stranger in San Francisco, for no reason at all. So, it would make sense then, if you believe in destiny (jury's still out!), that a lost, seventy-year-old letter would end up with me.

Los Angeles had been thrilling—but also overwhelming, and I was excited to be back in New York. I sifted through my pile of mail, relieved to be home, relieved to be doing anything mundane in my space, but disappointed as it seemed to be the usual suspects, junk mail and bills. More specifically, it was mostly advertisements for stuff I didn't need, stuff I didn't want, or stuff I couldn't afford, a casual reminder of exactly where I was in my life: Coupons for Buy Buy Baby? Nope. AARP membership information? I'll pass for now. A catalog for Bose sound systems? Thank you, but my studio apartment with French doors (fancy) leading directly into my...BED does not require *any* speakers as the square footage is so small the audio leaking from my headphones does the trick. That's how the Realtor should have sold it—who needs room for a sofa when it's so easy to fill the space with music?

I saved the Con Ed bill, the Design Within Reach (if your arm is a mile long) catalog as décor porn, and the Bed Bath & Beyond coupons for good measure—I had to stock up on trash bags to dump all this junk mail, so I might as well get 20 percent off. But then, just as I was about to toss the rest, an envelope caught my eye. I'd never seen one like this: an eight-by-ten envelope that was from the post office, like THE postal service, with a transparent window on the front that you could see through. Inside, there was a smaller, yellowed-with-age envelope with old-timey cursive handwriting. Not to put cursive in a category, but it was *grandparent* cursive. It's different, it's thoughtful, it's beautiful. They were taught to write more formally than we are now, and even though I remember practicing cursive as a kid, tracing the letters on worksheet pages, no one cared. There was no follow-through with handwriting. Am I from the last generation to even trace those cursive letters? Are children still taught handwriting?! I imagine kids nowadays come into school and set up mini cubicles, adjust their standing desks and writing tablets, everyone jacked up on five-hour energy shots, checking their social media in the middle of math class, taking selfies while their hologram teacher goes on about fractions in the background. I *clearly* don't have children. I'm jumping ahead (there aren't hologram teachers, right?), but handwriting feels almost ancient while we download and update by rote to the latest versions and systems and software. Everything is on screens now, and it all feels so immediate, and so fleeting. The more we rely on intangible pixels floating around, the harder it is to pinpoint like this: (1) I could brush it off. The postal service is clearly disorganized—they keep sending me elderly membership cards and diaper discounts. This letter slipped through the cracks—weird, but who cares? (2) I could tell a few friends and save the letter as a keepsake, a fun conversation starter. OR, (3) I could see this as an adventure, and follow the clues from an old piece of paper for no reason other than curiosity.

This felt like the type of thing that could only happen in New York City—a twist in time, a clumsy mistake in the system, a lost letter landing in the hands of a hopeless romantic. If that's not a movie (CONTACT MY AGENT) I don't know what is. The city, traced through the history of one apartment, one tenant to another. Maybe I romanticized it, maybe I blew it up into something bigger than it was, but this city has an energy, a lifeblood that beats and pulses and makes you feel like you're a part of something. I'd just gotten a seventy-year-old letter sent to me in the mail. I *was* a part of something! It felt like magic. On top of that, my grandmother Estelle was from Brooklyn, and grew up there in the '20s and '30s. I don't know a lot about her life in New York, but this made me feel closer to her—the date on the letter was only a few years after she would have lived there, and this couple was her age. I imagined what it might be like to see a correspondence from her back then, recirculated into existence. Who was she writing love letters to? What did she think about and worry about? Did she trudge up the stairs to her third-floor walk-up, looking through her stack of mail hoping for something good? Did she see the city like me, and wander the streets to lose herself in thought? Did she struggle with hair removal and what was the best and least painful way to go about it too? If her letter was out there, lost, I would want someone to find me.

So, I decided to Tom Hanks it. I *Cast Away*'d it. I WOULD DELIVER THIS LETTER IF IT KILLED ME!

When I knew I was going to deliver the letter, I got in touch with my friend Todd Bieber. Todd and I had known each other for a few years, we met auditioning for improv teams (neither of us got on one), but we'd hung out in the comedy community ever since. In 2011, while cross-country skiing during a blizzard in Prospect Park, he found a roll of film in the snow. He then documented his journey to find the people who owned the film; developing it and posting some of the images and information on where and when he found it online, imploring the internet for help. Thousands of people responded, and his project went viral. He traveled to Europe on a wild adventure, meeting new friends who offered to put him up in their apartments or take him out for drinks along his way. He documented his entire, inspiring experience. I remember watching his video online, it was so exciting—he made something incredible out of nothing, out of merely being curious. He returned the film to its rightful owners, but the story became way bigger than just them. He could have walked right past that film, not developed it, not given it a second thought, but he didn't. He saw a possible connection, something outside his normal life. I knew he was the guy to help me, I could be his next documentary about found things being returned.

Todd filmed me talking about the letter, about my hopes to find Joseph or Betty or their family, and about my excitement in general to begin whatever this was going to be. Maybe we would deliver the letter to an adorable old couple, living together in one of those tiny but perfectly lived-in New York apartments—the ones where every single thing in the room has its own story. Maybe there'd be photos of their family lined up on the mantel, evidence of their life since this letter was written? Maybe we'd get to see the love story closer to the end and then hear how it unfolded? You almost never get to see real love stories closer to the end.

Besides figuring out which songs this elderly couple and I would sing together accompanied by their in-home grand piano, and what pastries I'd bring along, the thing that interested me most about the letter was that it was *real*, and simple. I was so caught up in this false intimacy spending so much time online can provide, that this felt so pure. We were looking for two people and their family, simply to return something that belonged to them. I didn't want to rely on the internet, but rather try to find them the old-fashioned way, by foot, and see where we could go in the city to find information. I wanted that human contact even in the search process, the face-to-face interaction. So, Todd and I began our quest: We went to the municipal archives and scanned census records for my address, their names and any others mentioned in the letter itself. We went to the Greenwich Village Society for Historic Preservation and the New-York Historical Society library and talked to the employees there, but we kept coming up short—nothing led us to the family. After exhausting our in-person options, we went back online. We made a website, www.lostletterproject.com, Todd uploaded the video he'd shot of me, we posted it to all our social media platforms, and we asked for help the same way he had with his found roll of film. I remember watching the engagement happen in real time—people were spreading the story and commenting, it happened so fast!

Receiving a seventy-year-old letter in the mail somehow wasn't the most astounding part of this experience, but rather how people reacted when they read about my story. A lost love letter made people sit up, engage, want to help. It made them feel something. They excitedly shared our posts, commenting on Twitter, on Facebook, everywhere about the story, "Greenwich Village Woman Receives Letter Sent 70 Years Ago." I should also note, for the five and a half years I lived in Astoria dreaming about one day living in Greenwich Village, this headline made my life. The story got picked up by various news outlets online and was in the *NY Post*. My brother and sister-in-law called me—they were in a doctor's office waiting room and Kelly Ripa was holding the article from the *NY Post*, talking about my letter on *Live with Kelly and Michael*. Kelly didn't know me at the time (I was just a Greenwich Village woman!); this was before Kelly was on *Broad City*, before *Broad City* was on TV. She found it fascinating, a true New York story.

Random strangers had researched and were curious enough to band together and help me deliver this letter—and in only forty-eight hours! My romanticized idea of snail mail as this time-honored, tangible form of correspondence was put on pause—the internet can be kind, loving, and intimate too—we had found the family! The letter had been lost somewhere inside the US Postal Service, or floating around the country, behind countertops or hidden under a pile of paperwork for almost *seventy years*, and the internet found its rightful owners, in *forty-eight hours*! That's pretty inspiring. The end of the story doesn't quite match the beginning, but it wouldn't have left as lasting an impression on me if it had. Some of the best experiences don't end with a bang, but rather a dose of reality.

I didn't end up delivering the letter to an adorable old couple who invited us in for breakfast—no toast or jam—no telling us about their lovely relationship or what it was like to fall in love in my apartment on MacDougal Street. My heart didn't melt, seeing them together, holding hands after seventy years in their quaint but beautifully decorated apartment filled with Betty's original oil paintings as we sipped some rare tea they'd gotten years ago on vacation in India (my imagination really ran wild). There were none of those perfect, ribbon-wrapped images of what I imagined might happen.

I didn't deliver the letter to Joseph or Betty (they both had passed), but instead to their son, Scott, and his half sister Marna. Scott lived on the Upper West Side in Manhattan, only a subway ride away from my apartment, so not the travel-around-the-world-to-deliver-a-letter type of adventure I had hoped for. When I sat down with Scott and Marna, I finally heard their actual story: Joseph and Betty had gotten divorced a little over a year after Scott was born, leaving Joseph a single dad. Scott didn't have a relationship with his mom growing up, and only reconnected with her much later in life. This love story I'd been fantasizing about in my little apartment couldn't have been farther from the actual events. But the letter I delivered did give Scott an intimate look into his parents' brief love for one another when it was real. Neither Scott nor Marna had ever seen this side of their father, his delicate writing, his use of the word *God*, his soft side. It wasn't what *I'd* hoped for, but maybe it was something *they'd* needed.

Through whatever bizarre twist of fate, and postal service mishaps, I had ended up with a seventy-year-old letter on my kitchen counter, and I'd concocted a story. I wanted so badly to see real love play out, a story of two people that began right there in my apartment. But things don't usually unfold so gracefully: love, adventures, and in many cases, mail. We grow and change over time, just like our rapidly expanding ways of correspondence. We fuck up just like the post office. We idealize the past, fantasize about the future, and cross our fingers but more often than not, we get a punch in the gut. If I learned anything, it's that hopeless romantics don't give up after they get one seventy-year-old letter in the mail and it doesn't go as planned. Nothing is for sure, but it's all worth it, all the love lost and all the lost letters.

HEARTBREAK CITY

I had never been in love before.

I'd gotten to a certain point in my adult life where I felt that maybe I wasn't cut out for it. For this thing, this phenomenon that seemed to happen to everyone else. This monster that overtook my friends, my co-workers, random people on the subway, and swallowed them whole. I started to think my heart might be made of solid rock, impenetrable. I'd probably be written about later in life, a modern-day mystery, the woman who never fell in love. It would be my comeback! I'd stop doing laser hair removal and make it *really* interesting. I imagined a cross-country tour, Meet the Loveless Lady!—it would be just a few weeks though, as that type of thing can be pretty draining, especially in your seventies. I'd deal with logistics when the time came.

There was an underlying sense of loss within my body, for an experience I knew was essential to being alive. I was sad, but I shoved it away, pushed it under the day jobs, the random hookups, the comedy. Something was absent. I know this from my extensive study of love stories—first and foremost, the Rom Com. I love a solid Rom Com, in fact I have a hard time continuing my day after catching a glimpse of a Nora Ephron or Nancy Meyers film. A frame, a sound bite, the mere mention of one can hold me up. Entire flights where I needed to work have been sidetracked, calls canceled, important meetings have been delayed! I cry at the end of these films, when the two main characters finally get together—we knew they would! I'm a sucker for a good love story, a fated romance, basically anyone going out on *any* limb to declare *anything*. I have Spotify playlists completely devoted to love songs, ones I check periodically to make sure I haven't accidentally made public. I've lived vicariously through these films, these songs, through the pain and heartache, the triumphs, and the voice cracks. I was right there with them, but there's a difference between intellectually understanding love from a distance, and being inside it.

I couldn't pinpoint exactly what was wrong with me, what was off, why I wasn't able to connect on that level with another person. This connection seemed to come with great ease to everyone else. I felt disabled and ashamed. I thought if my skin were pulled back I'd be revealed to be the robot I was, unable to fully grasp the human beings around me. Don't get me wrong, I've been infatuated, had crushes, slept with, fucked, and dated many people in my life, but it always faded. I didn't and don't like wasting time with someone I know isn't for me, so nothing ever lasted very long. I'd end things swiftly, not engage fully. I've really liked a lot of people, even *loved* some, but I wasn't *in* love, hadn't found someone I really craved being with, anyone I saw as the other half of my team. I never felt a sense of togetherness, never that yearning to dive deeper. This was just how it was going to be, and I was starting to be okay with it.

A few years ago, one of my best friends said to me, nonchalantly, "I can't imagine you with anyone. You're so set in your ways." She didn't mean it to be harsh, but it was. I took her words about me in like a fugitive. Like a fugitive whose story you believe, but maybe no one else does yet, so you take them into your home, shove them into the closet with the water heater while the police search your block. Not like a killer! Like a wrongfully accused fugitive that wasn't dangerous or anything—you know what I mean. Anyway, I fed this thought, talked to it as I went to bed, lived with it for years. If one of my best friends, one of the people closest to me, honestly felt that she could never see me with anyone, maybe it was true? My friend was right, I couldn't imagine me with anyone either. I *was* set in my ways, I didn't know how else to be. I stopped hiding the secret (innocent) fugitive of an idea and embraced it. I brought it up out of the basement and started making coffee with it in the mornings, going on walks with it in the afternoons. Maybe things would be fine like this? I'd set myself up—I SHALL NEED NO ONE! I'd get huge, thick eyeglasses and an eclectic sense of style. I'd have a routine and stick to it. Plenty of people live like this, and I'd be just another stunning, single woman living it up into old age with nothing to care about but herself! Wonderful. My mind would spin out in other directions—shitty and somber directions. I pictured myself like the James Earl Jones character in *The Sandlot*, whispered about and feared, a mystery to the children in the neighborhood. I *had* been getting more involved in voice-over work—this was me, I was him, case closed!

And then, on a night like any other, I saw someone across the room at a party. It was someone I'd seen before, someone I already knew, but it was different. In one glance, I saw *her*, anew.

I'd only dated men up until this point. I was and still am attracted to guys, and always felt a natural inclination toward them, and it wasn't until art school that I ever even thought about being with a woman because that was the first time I was around out queer people.

I felt open, and figured if I ever met a woman I was interested in, I'd see what happened. But I didn't really put much thought into it, and I never felt that pang of desire, so I stuck with men. Looking back, I wish I had explored myself more thoroughly and found the beautiful parts of who I am that are attracted to the person, not the gender. I wish I'd questioned myself and the world I'd grown up in more. Every time I think I finally got it, finally figured myself out, I find there's more to unearth.

I've never been someone who fantasized about having the perfect wedding. I've never planned out my bridal party or imagined what my honeymoon might be like, and I still berate myself when I don't immediately, uncontrollably fawn over friends' engagement rings. "I'm sorry, it *is* gorgeous, I just forget to look at certain fingers for jewelry!" Those events and details aren't something I ever envisioned for myself as a kid, they weren't ever at the top of my to-do list. I was busy following my brother around, playing catch until it got too dark out. I was preoccupied daydreaming about being on *SNL*, or having a one-woman show on Broadway like *Gilda Live*. I was so caught up in dealing with what *I* might do, who *I* might grow up to be, I didn't even get into who I'd be with. I just assumed I would get married. I assumed I'd eventually marry an amazing guy who is funny, down to earth, creative, and successful, and then me and this handsome yet approachable guy would have kids. I just *assumed* that would play out, and so I pushed it into the future for whenever those cards might unfold. That *assumption*, that "norm," was just there, in my mind and body, for as long as I can remember. It's all I saw in my life, on TV, in movies, in school, everywhere I went. It's what you did and how you eventually ended up. This ingrained idea of one day having a heteronormative family wasn't something I was ever disgusted or hindered by, but rather a neutral and known fact, as clear as me growing up and getting a job.

Even in my adult life, after I moved to New York, getting married to a man and having kids was still just there, sitting somewhere in the distance, waiting for me to arrive after I found some success. But I'd started to move farther away from that story, not sure anymore if it was a place I was headed. I liked being casual in relationships, and the single recluse in me began to make herself comfortable. But I was distraught and insecure about my lack of connection in my love life, and the balance between my work and personal satisfaction was so uneven, it wasn't worth comparing. I felt helpless. I had to be more proactive, I had to do something to try and tip the balance the other way. So, on my thirtieth birthday, after a few drinks,

I made a decision, quietly and internally—from there on out, if I thought a dude was interesting or attractive, I was going to boldly ask him out. My first success was that very night, at a bar I'd invited friends to in Brooklyn. I'd always thought my friend Dan was cute, so I walked up to him and said casually: "I think you're adorable. Let me know if you'd ever want to get a drink. No pressure!" It worked! He said yes! What a fucking BADASS! This is still my go-to line by the way, and it usually works. Confidence is powerful and enlivening. I wasn't going to wait for guys to ask me out, to sweep me off my feet, because I knew that wasn't going to happen. I'd go out and do it myself. I had solved the "helpless" problem by taking matters into my own hands, but I still hadn't found connection.

So, there I was, two years later, at a friend's birthday party, mid-conversation with a sweet, cute guy I'd just met. I'd smile and nod at him, laughing with him at his jokes. I'd slip in the occasional, "Totally!" But I have no idea what he was talking about, what we were laughing at, or what I was saying "totally" in response to, because I found myself staring across the room, only seeing *her*. My mind shifted, an "aha moment" as my future best friend Oprah would say. The party ended and I went up to my hotel room. I remember sitting on the bed, trying to suss out the situation. I was clearly into her—I couldn't stop thinking about her! If she were a guy, there'd be no question what I would do. The only reason I wasn't asking her out was because she's a she. That seemed idiotic, to limit my heart based on gender. Maybe the things I always assumed would and should happen in my life were off, written by someone else. Maybe I would start over now.

So, I texted her.

And then, all the good parts happened. All the calls, the texts, the FaceTimes. The anticipation. All the uncontrollable smiles, the pings in my stomach. All the surprises, all the deep breaths, all the firsts. All the sweeping gestures, the tiny touches. The ease. The connection. The excitement, the laughter. All the plane tickets, the doors opening, the goodbyes, the notes left behind. All the hotel rooms and the playlists. The songs that made me think of her. The sharing of days, of frustrations, of fears. All the vulnerability I wasn't aware of. All the support and encouragement I didn't know I needed, the support and encouragement I didn't know I could provide. All the ways in which I wanted her to be proud to be with me, which turned into me being proud of myself. All the silence in the middle, all the hope. Full of hope. All the mornings, and the light. All the waiting for the coffee to finish, the learning about the coffee. All the late nights and the laughter. All the tucking of hair behind ears, the singing along to terrible songs in the car. The stupid dancing. And more laughter. All the times she smiled. All the times she smiled when she was looking at me. All the best things. There were other things in there, of course, the trickier things. The confusion, the disagreements, the lack of. The need for space and yearning for togetherness. The distance. The feeling like I wasn't good enough, the fear. All of those things and all of the others I can't try to write about. All of the things that make love impossible to explain. All the things I didn't understand before. It's all in there, the bad inside the good.

And then, it was abruptly over.

In the beginning of our relationship, right when we had started talking, me and her, I was alone and fainted in my apartment, smashing my face on my kitchen counter. MY NOSE WILL NEVER BE THE SAME BY THE WAY. I had taken a red-eye back from LA the night before and was dehydrated, or overworked—I still don't know exactly what happened. But right before I fell, as I was desperately trying to consume something, searching my fridge for anything to raise my blood sugar, I got this feeling throughout my whole body, this knowing sensation that I was no longer in control. *I was a goner.* I've felt that two more times since I ruined my beautiful nose:

A few weeks later, she was staying at a hotel in New York and we had gone to see a show. It was so early in us hanging out that we hadn't been telling everyone, except our close friends, like you do. I remember pretending to leave, hugging her goodbye in the lobby of her hotel, and walking outside with our friend we'd been having drinks with. I even scrolled my phone, feigning to call an Uber, complaining that it was taking forever. It's moments like this when I think to myself, *You know what, you are an exceptional actor!* It's never when I'm actually on set or at a table read, but rather when I'm blatantly lying to friends or acquaintances about something mundane. I SOLD THAT SHIT. This friend definitely thought my Uber was circling, because I was delivering quite the monologue about Ubers circling...I'm not gonna write it all out, because it was really more about the delivery, but it was Oscar-worthy. Actually...maybe just Globes-worthy. And my object-work with the phone!? Incredible. At least deserves a nomination! This friend finally decided to walk home, probably due to my play-by-play of Uber logistics, but I was free. When the coast was clear, I turned and went back into the hotel and took the elevator up to her room. I knocked on the door, smirking at my little play downstairs. The door opened and she pulled me inside. The ruse was over, we could be us again. She hugged me so tightly, held me there, and squeezed, like she might never let me go. I fell, completely out-of-control in love with this person, right then and there in that hug. In that hotel room. *I was a goner.*

And then, later, to the it-being-over thing. Being out of control *in* love is glorious. It's the feeling I wish for everyone, the unleashing of joy. The dual-skydive of glee into this unknown world of possibility. It's the closest thing we have to magic. But being out of control in heartbreak...? I wouldn't wish that upon anyone. It's unnerving, it's manic, it's hopeless. It's the most terrifying thing in the world for the person you love, who loves you back, to suddenly stop, to disappear, and not want to be in your life anymore. What do you do with that? I realized in the thick of this heartbreak that it wasn't only that I'd never felt this way about someone else, but no one had ever felt this way about *me*. I had never let anyone in this far, had never brought anyone home for the holidays before, had never let anyone fully see me. But I did, with her. Ooohh boy, *was I a goner.* I felt simultaneously like Russell Crowe in *A Beautiful Mind*, trying to connect the pieces of some unsolved math equation, and like Nell, isolated in a little cabin in my head, smack in the middle of the world as it always was.

So, I did what any intelligent, responsible, sane person would do.

I got a dog.

For a week.

I am an actual monster and should be put on garbage island to live out the rest of my days, floating in the middle of the ocean, building shelter from plastic bottles. That's next, right?

I should add that I took extremely good care of this puppy for the week she was mine. I wish I had simply fostered her, but the manic state I was in demanded wild, sweeping gestures, so I adopted her from a rescue. I took her to the vet and got all her medications. She wasn't used to a leash, but we were really making some progress in the house-training department. I got her set up with a trainer, had a dog walker and about every toy, bed, crate, and treat you could get a dog. When I knew I had to give her up, I brought her back to the foster mom I got her from and made sure she was safe and sound (with a carload of her new belongings). She is happy and healthy (I PROMISE SHE IS HAPPY AND HEALTHY), and I'm very certain I made the right decision. But I sometimes scroll through the photos from that week, of me with this puppy, and know I still belong on garbage island.

Even thinking about it now makes my stomach hurt. You know when you do something big, and in the moment, you're like, *I'm fine and this is right! Making this big change is appropriate, and I know exactly what I'm doing. I'm in control of my life and my actions and this is the thing for me! I'm an adult for crying out loud!* It was so clear, so ridiculously transparent, like all the biggest, boldest things are. I was trying desperately to move all my love that was now floating, up in the Cloud somewhere (clearly, still don't understand the Cloud), to this dog. To fill up my heart with this little puppy. I wanted so badly to have something, someone of my own to take care of. To *let* me take care of them, and it did not work. It wasn't like something just kind of not working. It was like having the adverse reaction to a sleeping medication, where instead of sleeping, you are anxious, jittery, and very much awake. Not sleeping at all! You might as well not have taken the medication in the first place. Sidenote: This is what happens to me every single time I try to take a different sleeping medication. I should really stop. But this dog, this adorable, perfect puppy, brought out a version of myself I had never been. Each cuddle sucked sadness out of my pores. My apartment became cramped, dark, tight with rage, with tears, with despair. The cutest eight pounds in the world made me fall apart anew. It was like a tipping point for me, crying-wise—you know that Malcolm Gladwell thing, the ten-thousand-hours rule—about how to be an expert at something you have to have practiced or worked at it for ten thousand hours. This dog and this week of crying was where I officially crossed over into being an actual depressed person—an expert crier. I'm here to say, and possibly toot my own horn, that it didn't take me the entire ten thousand hours, but I was indeed a professional tear maker. I was just that good. I'm a true Outlier of Tipping Points.

Everyone around me at the time could see that getting a dog was a terrible idea, catastrophic, but you can't tell people that. You have to let them live those mistakes. Did I mention I got her right in the middle of shooting Season 4 of *Broad City*? Maybe I delayed that reveal because it makes my decision even more idiotic and obvious. The shooting schedule of a television show is insane and unpredictable. Sometimes we shoot all night, from 5 p.m. to 5 a.m., and sleep all day. Sometimes it's the exact opposite. Sometimes we're shooting a scene that's supposed to be the dead of winter in the middle of the summer and sometimes we're stuck in a seven-foot hole in the middle of a cemetery for eight hours—shit is nuts! You have to be on the balls of your feet, ready for anything. Behind the scenes, there's a never-ending barrage of questions that need to be answered and possible outcomes that need to be anticipated. It's the type of thing Red Bull was created for. Personally, it becomes a selfish time; I hardly see friends or family, and weekends are usually used to catch up on sleep. While awake, most activities consist of finding new and unique places to sit. But I went ahead and I got this dog right in the middle of the chaos.

I could only operate normally when I was in work-mode. If there was too long a break between shots or meetings, I'd either veer into a zombie-like daze, or almost break down. I remember a scene we shot on the stage one night. It was a build of a closet in Ilana's new workplace, a restaurant called Sushi Mambeaux. While we were scouting at the location, a real restaurant in Williamsburg, we realized there wasn't a closet big enough for a few scenes we'd written, so we had to build a closet on the stage. In the scene, Ilana is suffering from depression (couldn't be more ironic for me at the time) and has been using a SAD (seasonal affective disorder) lamp to try and feel better throughout her shift. I remember waiting on the other side of the fake closet door while the crew finished setting up. There was some change in the shot and they were taking longer than usual to swap out a lens or get the lights just right. I was on the other side of that door by myself for too long, I'd slipped into the underbelly. I kept thinking of my new puppy, downstairs in the room where I got changed. I felt so lost, so incredibly low and numb, wishing some sort of SAD lamp would actually work for this. I felt a heaviness in my whole body, felt tears seep into the corners of my eyes and tried to push them away, frantically. There were forty people on the other side of that wall, specifically about to watch my face. *Stop, stop, stop thinking!* I yelled at myself in my head. And just as I was about to completely lose it, have to apologize to whoever and create an improvised lie about having something in my eye since lunch, the assistant director yelled, "Action," and without a second thought, I reached for the doorknob. I rushed into the scene in character, freaking out about my mom asking me how many people I've slept with. I will never forget that night and that week. How the show seems to always save me, and force me forward. How I have never been so raw, so out on a ledge before this time. How a beautiful, tiny little creature made me realize I can't do everything all at once.

I had never felt so untethered.

Besides the DOG week and its own turmoil, navigating my confusion and heartache felt like I was on a never-ending roller-coaster ride where everything related back to that. All the love songs, all the films, the poems, made sense now in a totally different way. Get outta here, Ephron—these people don't end up together, no one does! ADELE!? I GOT IT. ENOUGH! How could we all just be carrying on like this? I started looking at people differently—are they heartbroken too? Is that guy across from me on the subway also about to cry? I must be strong for him. If I cry, he'll break down and that wouldn't do either of us any good.

I had to find ways to distract myself from thinking about it, from replaying scenes from the relationship. I needed something to occupy my brain, entirely, and *Broad City* for me was perfect. But at night I was a complete and utter shit show. We're all always performing to the world, but when we get home and close the door to our apartments, or our bedrooms at night, the pain comes flooding back in. So, we have to distract ourselves again, right? TV! Movies! The internet! I tried to fill my head by reading or watching or listening to stuff. I watched shows, documentaries, old movies. I listened to albums I hadn't listened to from start to finish, caught up on podcasts I'd been recommended. I read novels and nonfiction, short stories, essays, and poetry. I even read a book about couples counseling—which made me feel terrible about not being in a couple, but is also something I quote almost constantly. It's called *Getting the Love You Want*, and I'm proud of myself for no longer being ashamed to tell anyone I read that book. I did order it on Amazon so no one would see me buying it in person, I have *some* self-respect!

I couldn't sleep and that amplified everything. It was like an alternate version of myself was let loose in my apartment each night—an angry person, a sad, lonely person. I was almost like Teen Wolf, but instead of when the moon comes out and I turn into a wolf, I'd turn into a wildly depressed person and also be a thirty-three-year-old woman instead of a teen boy. But my skin still looks like a teen and I too love a good bomber jacket. It was exhausting, just as I imagine being Teen Wolf was exhausting. I'm gonna be honest here and say that I don't think I've actually seen *Teen Wolf*, but I can gather the basic gist. Hiding something you're going through is intense and draining. But I just couldn't even deal with dealing with it, ya know? I would at some point, but these nights were like the fever you have to sweat out until it breaks and you're okay again. I feel like I should watch *Teen Wolf*?

The end of production was in sight. The process of editing is about two months and begins right after we're finished shooting. The edit is invigorating, challenging, and like a puzzle, filled with time and budget constraints. Sound design and visual effects come into play here and rejuvenate the whole show. It's where you see it all unfold. It's also a less stressful time, schedule-wise, as our main concern is getting what we've got to be exactly what we want. I was feeling a little bit more myself by the spring, but felt an underlying sense of anxiety. I was scattered and still just plain old sad. I'm an introvert by nature, but this was more than that. The nights were longer, leaving me more time to not-sleep. We weren't talking anymore at this point, me and her, and that distance and silence wasn't providing me any closure or relief. I started stressing about being finished editing, then what? I'd have time to only think about this? I'd be able to fully process where I'm at and how I've grown and how I really feel? What am I, crazy? I needed to leave and get as far away from my normal existence as I could, as soon as possible.

As a certifiable workaholic, I knew the only way I would

be able to get away and process this transformative relationship and the frustration I was still carrying around was if I created a project. So, I made a plan. We were scheduled to finish editing on the last day in June, Friday the thirtieth, and from then on, I had three weeks until I needed to be on the West Coast. I would leave Sunday, July 2, at the butt-crack of dawn and drive across the country to Los Angeles. Alone. That was what I would do. When my main distraction was set to end, I'd skip town and cook up another. This type of situation was exactly what horizons were there for, to drive right into.

I had a driver's license that didn't expire for years, and I was gonna use it! I didn't have any real goal besides finding time and space in which to be still and think. My vision of myself as an elderly, stylish, yet effortless Boo Radley had been tested. I was capable of love! Hooray! Now what? I had entered the world of pain and vulnerability and all the bullshit that comes along with it. I thought I'd been found, been discovered by someone, been wanted for exactly who I was, and now I felt like I might be a completely different person that I myself needed to find. I knew the past year had cracked me open and changed my assumptions of what my life could be. I wanted to create time to specifically think about that. To dive into the deep end as they say—in all the ways. I was a workaholic and didn't exactly know why. I had never fallen in love, and then I did. I had never been heartbroken, and now I was. I had never dated a woman before and now I was...dating women. For once, I wanted to put as much time into myself as I put into my work.

So, I did.

WATCH OUT
WILDERNESS

LISTS TO MAKE

- CLOTHES
- CAR STUFF
- HOTEL / TRAVEL ITINERARY
- GEAR
- WHAT TO DOWNLOAD TO LISTEN TO
- THINGS TO DO AT APARTMENT
  BEFORE I LEAVE
- BEST BAGELS
- FIRST AID / EMERGENCY STUFF
- TOILETRIES TO GET

- MY INTENTIONS

OPRAH

JUST BECAUSE I CAN

NEW YORK CITY → ASHEVILLE, NC
DRIVE TIME: 12h 17min

RULES OF CONDUCT

Wear sunscreen, especially on left arm.

Call parents, assure them you are fine.

Stay hydrated.

Stick to the plan but try to allow room for spontaneity.

Do not listen to Bonnie Raitt's "I Can't Make You Love Me."
Ever. Don't even think about this song.

Try to find ways to move your body. Sitting in a car for 5–10
hours a day isn't part of your health plan.

Try local fare, but don't go NUTS.

Follow your gut.

Follow your gut into even the rest stop bathroom. Not shitting when you have to shit is bad news. Get it out of your system, like everything else.

Bring Purell.

Do not listen to Sia's "Breathe Me." If you must, do not be driving, especially not in a beautiful landscape. If you are, and it plays, *do not* by any means put your window down and picture your car driving through the expansive terrain from an aerial drone shot.

If Bonnie Raitt's "I Can't Make You Love Me" somehow plays by accident, immediately play "Nick of Time," right after. You might be all right.

No texting and driving.

Try not to work. This is your break. Try not to work.

If you do end up getting an idea, write it down, but for later, after the trip.

Don't drive at night if you can help it.

Scope out hotel pools before going in. There are too many articles about kids shitting in hotel pools. Beware.

Learn one new word a day on the new app. Try to use in conversation.

Avoid becoming *irascible* by little things along the way. Take them as they come and move on.

Find silence wherever you can.

Don't pull a Thelma and Louise.

DAN

ASHEVILLE BED-AND-BREAKFAST

My main objective was to get as far away as soon as possible, so on day 1 of this solo journey outward and inward, I drove all the way to Asheville, North Carolina. Which, if you stop for lunch in Baltimore and briefly wander the blocks of your alma mater, is roughly a twelve-hour drive.

I landed at my bed-and-breakfast at about 10 p.m., and it was everything I had imagined: chimes hanging down from the Victorian carport, a massive veranda with *multiple* rocking chairs, and homemade sweets, kept fresh under Saran Wrap on the table in the foyer. It was old-fashioned, with wood finishes and cozy knickknacks the owners probably collected over the course of their life together. The friendly woman that was there late to meet me gave me my keys and showed me to my room. They were actual keys! A large, clunky, old-school key was for the front door, and another actual key was for my room— not one of those plastic electronic touch-cards that hardly ever work on the first try. So far, this was *exactly* like *Gilmore Girls*.

Gilmore Girls was my main reference point for bed-and-breakfasts—I'd never stayed in one, but I had heard Asheville was full of verandas, and that led me directly to my Sookie and Lorelai fantasy—I'd stay in a B&B! I can talk fast if I really try, and I already drink heaping amounts of coffee! This was what I needed—to be thrown into a house full of strangers, homemade jam, and, fingers crossed, an available rocking chair. I wondered what weird characters I'd run into while dodging those double swinging doors into the kitchen? Which type of produce would be overdelivered, forcing the chef to have to create an entire menu using only zucchini!? Which handyman was hooking up with which housekeeper? Would a mysterious package arrive and they'd have to figure out who it was for? Could it be for me!?

I never watched *Gilmore Girls* when it aired, I binged it on Netflix only a few years ago. It was that comforting fantastical nostalgia for the early 2000s that hooked me, the will-they-won't-they between Lorelai and Luke—SIDENOTE, "will-they-won't-theys" are always WILL-THEYS, right?! They *will* end up together. It's exhausting, but we fall for it every time: "The timing for them just isn't right…" or "they're so great to-gether, but she has to focus on work—makes sense." But we *know*. We knew the whole time! If you're in a real-life "will-they-won't-they" scenario, are you aware of it? Do you think Ross-and-Rachel situations are happening all over the place? Maybe I should try to get in one of these will-they-won't-theys? It seems way more dramatic than my everyday life, full of stolen glances, passionate handwritten apologies, and hours spent staring longingly out of windows as it rains outside. I hardly ever spend full hours staring out windows, but maybe I should. Maybe my Rachel or Ross is out there staring longingly thinking about me? Wow. Maybe my new confused and noncommittal romance will begin right here at this B&B...? Their dog could steal my shoe and I'd have to chase it around the property, or I'd choke on a hot zucchini croquette and they'd give me the Heimlich—so many meet-cute, will-they-won't-they opportunities!

My room was the corner, at the top of the stairs, with a big bay window, a claw-foot tub, and creaky wooden floors that felt "authentic," which, when dealing with floors, is important. Some wood floors, even though they are wood, are just bullshit, right? It's like...these are fake? Someone has gone out of their way to make these floors seem wooden, and they might technically be, but you're not fooling anyone. They're dipped in plastic gloss and have been manufactured up the wazoo. Those wood floors are basically the equivalent of an Oreo being considered food. Yeah, I can ingest it, *like* food...but it ain't the real deal. Long story short, the room was quaint and adorable. There were ample nooks and crannies filled with books about Asheville's local history, recommendations on where to eat in town. A special-seeming chocolate was in a dish on the nightstand. I was so tired from the drive, I got in bed almost immediately, staring up at the painted vaulted ceiling—a mural of the Blue Ridge Mountains. I was doing it, putting myself out there in this new interesting place. I fell asleep picturing the beautiful and impeccably stacked homemade blackberry scones in store for me tomorrow morning at breakfast. Or rhubarb. Or...both!

And with the first light of the morning sun—I shot up in bed:

MOTHERFUCKER!

They didn't own and operate a *bed-and-breakfast* in *Gilmore Girls*, it was an *inn*! It was the Dragonfly INN!

What have I done?

Right. Bed-and-breakfasts aren't where you go to be alone, or to make space and room in which to process what may or may not, later in life, be considered one of the most transformational years in your entire existence! No! You don't do that. The mere mention of staying at a bed-and-breakfast makes some people uncomfortable—it did when I told them! It's not like a hotel, it's more intimate, friendlier, upbeat, and inviting. I wasn't currently any of those things—what was I thinking? I don't even like people that much. I prefer being left alone, I'm hit or miss with small talk, and awkwardly trying to make myself at home in a stranger's house is close to being my worst nightmare. I don't want to insert myself into the drama about the zucchini! What the fuck am I doing at a bed-and-breakfast?

Okay. All right. This was going to be fine. In some night sweat, Google-search-fever-dream, I apparently made the wrong call about my lodging situation, but if anything, the breakfast had to be good. I'd figure out the rest of my day later, but I hadn't eaten anything since the hard-to-swallow nut bar in the car last night—I needed coffee, badly, and I was going to find those homemade scones.

I could hear rumblings of other guests downstairs as I opened my door. *Be cool. It's fine, smile and just be friendly.* In my hesitation to rush downstairs, I almost forgot to lock my door—right, I have to lock it. All of a sudden I felt like a kid, upstairs in my house, listening for activity down in the kitchen, locking my room before I left for school. I would never have done that though—I'd never locked my room in any apartment I'd shared, and both my childhood bedrooms never had locks, not even on the inside. My main childhood bedroom—what would later be "my mom's house"—had Pepto-Bismol–pink walls with plush, turquoise carpeting, colors that would drive an adult insane—granted my parents did choose the colors, so who knows. The built-in shelves on the wall above my trundle bed were filled with books and my extensive collection of troll dolls. What a terrifying toy to collect. The thought of that shelf now feels like the preface of a nightmare, or the beginning of a *Law & Order* episode—before they find the body, someone screaming as we pan across fluorescent troll hair. But I was enamored of these little monsters, and I should specify that I was into the *old* version of trolls, the originals—they were redesigned at a certain point, and I could tell the difference. No one else seemed to be able to spot the detail in the texture of the plastic or whatever material their bodies were molded from, but I could. I'd hate to call myself a troll expert, but at the time, I guess I was. If you take anything from this anecdote, let it be my eye for design.

I'm going to go farther away from the B&B for a moment, because tangents are the most effective way I have to stall going to what I feel might be an extremely uncomfortable breakfast full of me halfheartedly making small talk over mediocre pastries. This pink childhood bedroom of mine was the first place that felt like my own, but as I became a teenager, I started to feel like I needed more privacy. Because there wasn't a lock, and asking for one to be installed seemed like an acknowledgment of guilt, I'd hide things all over the room to feel like I had more control over my space. I'd slip my journal under the bed, out of sight. I don't even know what I was hiding. At fourteen, I had zero secrets, definitely nothing good enough to hide—I think for a time, a lot of my journals were about championing a drug-free lifestyle, which I eventually, if you've followed my work over the years, veered from ever so slightly. I imagine my mom or dad finding this journal, looking for juicy sex stories or catching tales of me sneaking out to crazy parties, only to find how strongly I was inspired by the D.A.R.E. initiative. The entries eventually got juicy though, don't you worry about me . . . I did pretty good. As I got older, and moved away from D.A.R.E. into the Truth or Dare, hiding weed around my room proved to be my main challenge and priority. I'd bury it in drawers, inside shoes, packed away in backpack pockets, but these all felt too exposed. Not to mention the smell. The smell gave it away. And then finally, on a day like any other, a hiding spot came to me like an epiphany sent from God herself: my Kiddush cup.

My Kiddush cup was given to me by my synagogue when I had my Bat Mitzvah, the one gift I held on to because it seemed significant. It was metal or brass and drinking anything out of it made that liquid more important. I should mention that the Kiddush cup is used to sanctify Shabbat and other Jewish holidays and is for wine (or grape juice), and not a crazy cup in which you're intended to test out other liquids to see if they feel more "holy." But being Jewish is all about asking questions, and my curiosity was piqued: Did water become holy because it was in the cup? Would it be okay to put ice in it? Would I dare use it to eat ice cream out of? Would people be intimidated if I was using the cup in a casual manner at the kitchen table? And it wasn't just the cup that felt significant, it was also its container. It came in a purple velvet box with a cutout inside fitted perfectly for the cup. As I was examining the scope of my room for the ideal place to stash my...stash, it came to me: I could hide weed in the cup itself, so even when the box was opened, you couldn't see it. It was truly a holy experience. I realize this confession is intense for some, extremely enlightening for others, and possibly sacrilegious for many, and I'm okay finding that middle ground. I needed a safe space and found it in my Kiddush cup. I feel as though my rabbi would somehow be proud that my weed was consistently sanctified.

My privacy is even more sacred now, although I'm certainly sharing more of myself in my work than I ever have. Staying at this B&B instead of a hotel all of a sudden felt like a loss of privacy, and locking this door was all I had left between me and whoever was downstairs. Would I be able to have whatever shitty scones they had in peace? Should I try to bring my meal back up to my room—that seems like it'd be frowned upon at a bed-and-breakfast. And then, just as I realized I was still standing in the hall, quietly weighing my options, I noticed the door of another guest room ajar. I couldn't help but take a peek inside. Of course, nothing was out of the ordinary—when doors are left open like that, there's never something going on. Never an open briefcase full of cash, never a bloody knife dripping down on the saucer, which I believe is what the rules and guidelines of saucers and spoons are, it just creates a mess. The spoon has just been stirred around in the coffee and now it's just going to drip into the divot of the saucer so every time you lift the cup, the bottom is soaking wet because it's filled with coffee the spoon brought in. We could blame it on the spoon, but I firmly believe in the importance of the spoon so I'm not going there. I'm just saying what we're all thinking. I know this is controversial (typical bed-and-breakfast controversy here), but I just don't feel like we need saucers. THERE, I said it.

I took a few sips and refilled my tiny floral painted, bullshit coffee cup and found a small table by the wall. You ever try to carry a full cup of coffee by the saucer? You thought I was finished with this and apparently, I'm not. The sound alone is enough to drive you mad, the clanking of ceramic against ceramic, hinting at an inevitable spill, a future crash on the floor, havoc! This is the type of thing I linger on for too long.

The table itself was covered with glasses, so many plates, too many knives. The proper table setting. Bed-and-breakfasts seem to be one of the last places on earth that hold fast to the traditions of fine dining. We shall use all the silverware, have courses, be dignified! I sat there in jean shorts, a T-shirt, and Tevas. I don't *usually* wear Tevas—I thought there might be water involved at some point along my trip, me walking into water to be more specific, and I could think of no better option than Tevas. While I waited for a menu that never came (bed-and-breakfasts apparently don't have menus), I scoped out the dining room and remembered something I often forget until it's staring me in the face: I was by myself at a place where one usually isn't. The mediocre small talk I was anxiously anticipating upstairs wouldn't have been a thing if I was with someone—because I'd be making terrible conversation with *them*. And then I took a closer look at the dining room and an even more obvious realization came over me: *Right*. Bed-and-breakfasts are a thing couples do. *Wonderfuckingful.* I sat there alone, my main relationship at the moment being the passive-aggressive situation with my cup and saucer, in a room full of people staring into each other's eyes, weaving their arms through the many glasses that covered their tabletops to hold hands.

Breakfast at a bed-and-breakfast as a single person traveling alone is not great. It's not something I would highly recommend. It's as if you're struggling to lift a fancy coffee cup up to your mouth, with a spotlight directly on you. The sound of your fingers trying desperately to fit through the tiny handle, amplified so other conversations can't continue. People looking in your direction. Small gasps, horror! This is what fueled my inner dialogue, one side arguing how stupid I'd been to make this choice, and the other worrying what those other people, those pairs might think of me there, alone.

In reality, no one was glaring or shooting me looks. But I stood out. I didn't fit in with the dining room of couples on their romantic getaways. I had gotten so caught up in the delight of the bed-and-breakfast (an inn) I'd seen on TV, I forgot to actually picture myself there in that situation. I'd gone from imagining meet-cutes on the front porch, to worrying about making small talk, to now feeling insecure about being the only single person in sight. I eat out alone all the time, and never feel this pang of uncomfortable social anxiety. But in heightened, coupled-off scenarios like weddings, holidays, vacations, and now bed-and-breakfasts, in my own mind, the fact that I am alone becomes the most significant thing about me. Which is why I tend to avoid them.

This fantasy, this projection I was throwing into the dining room was part of the social narrative I had seen forever, one I try to stop reciting. A young-ish single woman alone in a bed-and-breakfast is seen as inherently pathetic—instead of incredibly empowering. A man on my same road trip would be viewed as a cool loner, figuring himself out as he explored the vast roads of our beautiful country. There are no projections about the men, no questions, no pity. As insecure as I can get about this narrative, about what people might be thinking of me, it is drastically overpowered by a sounding alarm I've installed that blares: DO NOT GIVE A FUCK!

And if women ever do *dare* to risk the humiliating experience of eating alone, we better do it right! I remember an episode of *Sex and the City* where beautiful music swells as we pull back on Samantha, eating by herself in a bustling New York City restaurant. The empowering message we were sold was that she was completely alone without distraction—no book or anything to occupy her attention or keep her company, because those things take away from being truly oneself. She was proudly owning the *horrific* experience of a meal on one's own. I get it, when you don't have something to work on or to read it's a totally different story, you are completely exposed. But why is that the only way to own your independence? Why is *that* the brave moment? A man's self-confidence and independence are never called into question when he's reading at dinner! Call me crazy, but I usually read...alone? I write alone, I think alone. Just because you have shit to do and want to *also* eat out at a delicious restaurant while you're taking care of business, doesn't mean you aren't as independent or comfortable with yourself. I say bring your fucking library out with you and *own* that. Do whatever you want. You don't have to sit silently, chewing each bite fifty times or whatever you're supposed to do to digest properly, and stare out into the masses of people interacting with each other to be comfortable with being alone. Now we can pull away slowly as beautiful music swells.

Maybe I had to stay at that bed-and-breakfast to clarify what my personal preferences are, to realize how much I value my privacy, and to get a wake-up call that TV shows are not reality. You'd think I'd know that by now, but the suspension of disbelief can be strong when we are at our weakest. I ended up talking to one of the owners for about an hour as I ate breakfast, a man in his late sixties who owned the B&B with his wife. He told me about his family, stories about how he ended up in Asheville. This was his second life, he started over again with this bed-and-breakfast. He asked me where I was going, and when I said California, he told me all about when he lived there in his early twenties with a bunch of friends, surfing and trying to figure himself out. As he spoke, the old-fashioned wood finishing and the decorative knickknacks became charming again, the coffee was delicious, the keys in my pocket were weirdly massaging an area on my hip that needed it. I'd make the most of this place, and there was a rocking chair with my name on it.

But there weren't *any* scones.

HOT-BUTTON ITEM

CANNED
MANDARIN
ORANGES

FIGS IN NEW FRIEND'S CAR
ON THE WAY TO HIKE THE
BLUE RIDGE MOUNTAINS

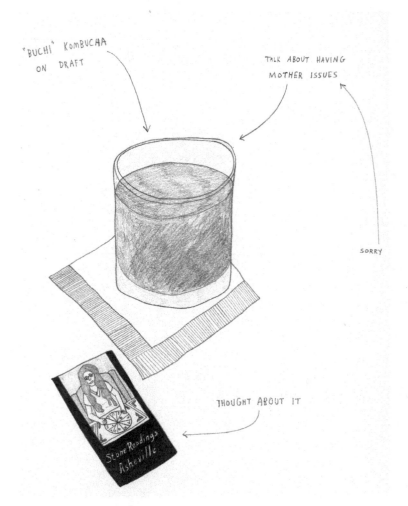

"BUCHI" KOMBUCHA ON DRAFT

TALK ABOUT HAVING MOTHER ISSUES

SORRY

THOUGHT ABOUT IT

THE BIG QUESTIONS

Is it worse to be accidentally walked in on while using a public restroom or to be the one who accidentally walks in on someone else?

If we're being monitored by the government from satellites, how many people are simultaneously taking selfies? Or rather, taking four or five selfies until they get a good one.

Why does the default song on your phone that plays automatically when you start your car always have to be something that drives you crazy?

Why does the sight of the person you're in love with, wearing your clothes, feel so deeply good?

Are we living in a computer simulation or what?

At what point are ankles considered cankles? Is there a chart to reference?

What are the new tipping guidelines? How much am I supposed to tip when I've ordered something to-go, or just bought something off a shelf? They have those new credit card / chip reader machines that automatically only give you options to tip 15 or 20 percent. Do I have to tip if I'm buying a box of crackers off a shelf? No one helped me with the crackers. Are we just tipping all the time for everything now? No judgment, but just curious if that is now the norm?

Do SAT scores matter now?

What happens to all the cars—there's got to be a massive amount of discarded and unsold cars somewhere, right?

Do any relationships ever actually last?

Why does the pen they give you to sign the check or the important document never work? Why does it work for them when they take it back and try it themselves?

Why do so many people hate women?

Why do we continue to measure things with our arms, feet, fingers, etc.? There are so many tools now for measuring.

When people arrange stuffed animals in the back of their cars, is it for us, or them?

Is there a point in time when you stop feeling like you're eighteen?

Will anyone invent a solution that prevents the drawstring within the hood of a hoodie from falling out in the wash, and thus never, ever being able to be put back through the hoodie-hole? Where is our savior? We're all waiting, patiently.

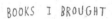

BOOKS I BROUGHT

FINALLY, I KNOW

SPONTANEOUS, POSSIBLY ANXIOUS PURCHASE

C.J. CREGG

THE WEST WING = 4TH OF JULY PARTY

MEMPHIS SLEEP STUDY

Alarm set on phone: 7:00 a.m.
Do Not Disturb: on
Brainwaves App: Set to—LIGHT RAIN—for 30 minutes
Lights: off

10:04 p.m.

I can't believe how much it's raining, I don't remember ever being in a rainstorm like this, and it's been going on for hours!

It is nice though, at least from inside.

I forgot about rain and thunder, how nice it can be. It was such a big part of my life as a kid, during the summers at camp it felt like you were a part of the storm, but I guess since I moved to New York, rainstorms have just become a nuisance. Rain in the city is the worst, at least when you're commuting or going…anywhere. My shoes and socks get soaking wet and the water always kicks up all over the back of my pants.

Does that happen to everyone or maybe it's just how I walk? I've never asked anyone else about this. I have to remember to ask someone. I wonder if the sock thing happens to everyone too, or maybe I'm the only one whose socks slip down under my feet when walking around in rain boots? I always have to readjust. It's the worst when I'm walking with someone— I hate making people stop because of a shoe or sock issue. I can't be the only one this happens to! I *know* I'm not the only one with umbrella issues, the wind blowing them inside out. There's nothing more embarrassing than an intersection full of strangers watching you cross the street in a storm, trying to flip the umbrella back to its original shape. This does happen to me a lot...I wonder if the statistics are the same for me and other people with regard to umbrellas? I have to look into it.

It's nice right now though, the rain. This is actually the exact sound my phone is replicating to help me go to sleep. Wait, is this partially my phone? Yes. The phone is making rain sounds. I guess I don't need the Brainwaves tonight. Like it works anyway.

Maybe because it's the real thing I'll be able to go to sleep and stay asleep? Yeah, this is going to work, hundreds of sound machines and apps are made to specifically replicate this natural sound. I'm going to shut my eyes and sleep through the night!

10:22 p.m.

This fucking top sheet. How do people sleep when this top

sheet is tucked in so tightly? I can't even fit my feet under here. Why do they always make it so tight? I guess the bed is supposed to look nice and made when you come in, and then it just gets ruined on a daily basis. What a stupid thing to be annoyed about, the top sheet. People are suffering in the world, everywhere, in terrible ways, and I'm in a hotel bed, annoyed at my fucking top sheet. What an asshole.

10:45 p.m.

I have to switch positions. I'll probably fall asleep on my side. Yeah, definitely my side. I can't believe I need a fucking pillow next to me to hug, but it's happening. No one's here to see it, it's fine. It does feel better, more comfortable. It's nice to know it's here—like if I move, or toss and turn, it's there, touching my back or my leg, *almost* like someone's back or leg would. Ugh, this isn't a person, it's a hotel pillow, probably covered in germs and who knows what else! I know what's happening here, I'm not under the presumption that the pillow is anything more than what it is—just a pillow next to me in bed, comforting me with its touch. There's nothing to be ashamed of, it's fine, and okay, and completely normal.

The pillow has become too much of my story. The pillow isn't significant in my life—this is a random pillow that I will never see again after tonight, and I have no relationship to it. Stop thinking about the pillow and how it's *not* a person!

10:52 p.m.

I gotta move.

11:06 p.m.

The West Wing, wow. What a gang. It feels good to watch it now, in this political climate. It's comforting. Even though that episode was about the characters dealing with the aftermath of an assassination attempt, it's still a soothing show right now. Allison Janney. Man, she's great. Such a phenomenal actor, able to straddle comedy and drama, she holds her own with a cast of mostly men. They're all great though, a true ensemble... I did just hear some crazy thing about Martin Sheen making a documentary about O.J. being innocent... that doesn't sound like Jed Bartlet, but he's a fictional character. That can't be what it's really like to work at the White House. Surely not now...

11:22 p.m.

Ugh, I have to readjust. Maybe being on my back will be better? Yeah, like a horizontal tree pose.
Okay, yeah, this is more comfortable.

Rogue fireworks are still going off?? It sucks it was raining too hard to see any earlier, but they had to have canceled the big ceremony? But maybe I missed it? Maybe people just stayed down there on the main drag and stood with their umbrellas watching the fireworks? I doubt it. I made the right call coming back to the hotel. Yeah, there's no way. Even if people did stay down there—they'd all be gathered around with their umbrellas—you couldn't even see the sky! Ohh man—that's hilarious, if there was a crowd gathered for fireworks and everyone had an umbrella. That's good. I gotta write that down.

Crowd gathers at fireworks display with umbrellas (can't see sky)

I don't know why I even wrote that last part. It's obvious a crowd wouldn't be able see the sky with umbrellas—why did I write the explanation of the joke for myself? I should delete it. But then again—maybe I won't open up that note on my phone for a while—like months or years from now, and when I do I won't remember what I was talking about. I might not understand my sense of humor whenever I read it next. What if something happens to me, and my loved ones or the person who finds me are looking through my phone and they come across that note? They might need the explanation to get it visually. I wouldn't want to be dead and for my notes to not make sense. I'm going to leave it.

11:40 p.m.

The fireworks are *finally* starting to die down. And they sound pretty far away. I guess it's *the* night for fireworks, so it makes sense that people really go all out. Even though it feels off to be celebrating our country right now—or at least not by rote—not because we're told to. The Fourth of July doesn't feel too good this year. I'm happy it stormed. That feels appropriate. Most of the holidays we have in place are outdated. They need to be completely overhauled. What are we even doing? National holidays just showing up in my calendar on my computer—it's just like the U2 album. Like, I'm okay. I'll make this decision on my own, thank you very much.

We should have fireworks displays when things change *now*, not just to commemorate past events that have been told to us through a patriarchal lens. Not to celebrate quarter-truths and bullshit dates on the calendar. Yeah!

Who are you fucking talking to?

11:54 p.m.

I guess you can just go and buy fireworks and...set them off? I've never had the desire to do that. It feels inherently dangerous, and the payoff doesn't seem worth it. You probably need to stand very close to the firework, and by the time you light it, there's no way you'd be able to run far enough away to really appreciate the firework in the sky. And I love fireworks—but I wouldn't want to go through all the trouble of buying them and almost getting my arm blown off, and then not even get the chance to appreciate them. Maybe I'm wrong? Maybe there's a long rope you light with a match, like an old-timey cartoon, and it travels a distance to set it off? I'd do that, I'd light that rope. Those ropes always provided such suspense.

How were fireworks invented? Probably an accident at first. They must have been reworked over and over again and built to fly straight up and blow up in different ways and be perfectly timed. How many people in the world have the job of engineering fireworks displays? There's gotta be one in every city, or maybe there are only a few and their designs are used all over the world. Wow, I bet there's only a few of them. Have I ever met one? I'd like to. I'm gonna look into this when I get up.

Should I write that down?

No. If I was meant to remember trying to meet a fireworks person, I will. I'm going to leave this one up to fate. Me meeting a fireworks engineer.

12:07 a.m.

Too much light is coming from the sliver beneath the bathroom door.

It's fine.
Just ignore it, it's not that much light.

Fuck me. Why can't I just let this go? I wish I was someone who could leave this be.

I can't. I must get rid of the light.

Okay. I've dealt with all the things that were clearly preventing me from sleeping:
I fixed the blinds, I peed and shut the bathroom door so no light comes through.
There's...yep, no more light seeping in.
I can fall asleep now, it was definitely the sliver of light keeping me up.
Great.
Perfect.

12:18 a.m.

It is nice to have small problems that you can fix immediately, like getting rid of the light coming into the room. Some problems are so big, they take forever to make any progress. Work problems require so many discussions, so many emails back and forth, so many revisions to a script or tweaks the process, and sometimes they never even get fixed, just sort of talked through. Addressing a personal issue and trying to figure out how to make significant growth can take years! I think?! I hope! It's nice to be able to make a quick change and solve a problem immediately!

It was just light coming in from the bathroom...Shut. Up!

12:27 a.m.

It's kinda hot in here now, I have to pull one leg out from under the covers.

It's crazy how that light coming through the bathroom door bothered me *even* through my shut eyelids...Maybe I have super-sight? My astigmatism doesn't change my eyesight that much, but maybe my eyes are shaped in some way that makes them uber-sensitive, able to detect small shifts in light patterns or whatever hard-to-see things are called?!?

Hmm. Are people who have had Lasik more sensitive to light? Lasik really changed the game, eye-wise. I wonder what will be next? Maybe it will be to shape eyeballs in weird ways or something, so we can see farther or through stuff?

12:40 a.m.

Shit, my shoulder again. Maybe it's bothering me more because I'm sitting so much in the car? I should get a massage at some point on this trip. Me trying to massage my own shoulder isn't doing me any good.

It's twelve forty-one, great. I have to be up in six hours if I'm going to leave on schedule. I guess it's my own schedule...No one is holding me to it. But I made the schedule for a reason! I can't just start abandoning the plan left and right! I'm only on day 4. I made this plan, I should try to stick to it.

I'm gonna fall asleep any minute and it'll be fine.

12:49 a.m.

Those girls from high school were so nuts, bragging about how much they stole from Abercrombie & Fitch. I still can't believe it. Bananas!

Why am I thinking about Abercrombie & Fitch and those girls? Could that *be* more random.

Hahaha Chandler.

But coats and sweaters!? They'd steal huge hauls at a time, just bring it all into the dressing room and wear it all out! They must have figured out how to take the plastic security sensor off the clothes. I could never do that. I'd probably throw up in the dressing room in the middle of the theft, then I'd have to buy all the stuff I was trying to steal because I just threw up all over it. I wouldn't be able to wear any of the items out because they'd be disgusting. I'd probably look sick, and maybe the manager of the store would feel bad for me and not make me pay. I'm terrible at talking to managers, especially of retail stores, especially when I was a teenager! I don't even know what I'd do, bring the "tampered with" merchandise up to the register and try to explain? I'd have to act sick, like really sick. I guess if I threw up, I'd feel sick, but I'd have to amp it up. I could do that...But what if there are other customers up there, waiting to pay and they leave because some crazy girl is walking around with foul-smelling clothes?! Would I be responsible for the store losing even more business? And then there's the dressing room! I think about some girl going in after me. Ohh, man. Good thing I never tried to steal clothes.

1:08 a.m.

I cannot get comfortable. No position feels right, fuck. Okay, just lie on your back and breathe through your mouth.

She told me that.
Right.
I couldn't sleep one night, and she turned to me and said gently, "Lie on your back and breathe through your mouth."

It kind of feels like she just said it, like she's here with me.

1:13 a.m.

Stop!
Stopstopstopstopstopstopstopstopstop!
Why'd you have to think about her? Find something else to think about.

Think. Think. Think. Anything else.

The drive. Okay, right.
Ten-hour drive tomorrow. Today. Ten-hour drive today. It'll be fine. I just want to try to make it to Austin before it gets too dark.

1:25 a.m.

Sleep. I will fall asleep...NOW!

Okay, just focus on your breath.
Lie on your back and breathe through your mouth.

I should try meditation. Everyone says that. TM. That's what they all say to try. I did read the David Lynch book about TM. I should check it out tomorrow, the program everyone talks about. I'll remember.

1:33 a.m.

It's so weird to sleep in a random bed, in a city I've never been to before and one I'll leave again tomorrow. I've had so many beds in different cities. Maybe if I shut my eyes and imagine myself in all my other beds it'll be like counting sheep?

Okay, focus.

Close your eyes and think of your past beds.

Imagine being under the covers in all those other beds. This is good, this'll work.

My childhood beds...

The pink and purple covers at my mom's house, the cold bars of the trundle bed just next to me...

The metal Ikea bed frame with a denim blanket and T-shirt sheets at my dad's house...

The beds at camp—the tiny cots with wire springs that would squeak when you sat on them...

The bed in my dorm room, with drawers built in, shoved into a corner next to the wall of concrete blocks...

My beds in Baltimore in my studio apartments, bundled with blankets when the heat wasn't working...

My bed in Boston looking at windows onto Commonwealth Avenue, the bustle of cars passing by outside...

Friends' beds...

Beds in my Astoria apartments...

Lovers' beds...

My bed on MacDougal...

My bed on Hunts Lane...

Her bed—FUCK!

Jesus.

1:51 a.m.

Think of something else! Think of anything else... gas, gas! Yes, I have to get gas tomorrow on my way out of Memphis. Great.

I'll look it up when I wake up—where the closest gas station is. Ugh, what an idiot, pulling into the pump on the wrong side. I've done it like three times? It's a good thing no one is with me to witness that. Why is it so hard for me to remember what side the gas tank is on!? I don't drive all the time, it's okay. Different cars have different sides. I should be easier on myself. At least I don't use my cell phone while I pump gas. Is that even a real thing? Where did I hear about that? Is using your cell while pumping gas the worst thing you can do? I swear I heard that somewhere. There are so many "worst" things you can do.

2:03 a.m.

I'm chilly now—all extremities have to get under the covers.
...Where's the pillow? Ohh there, just touching my leg a tiny bit.

That's better.

2:15 a.m.

Ohh wow, this is a nice ceiling, what a unique texture. You don't see that often.

I'M TERRIBLE AT HANDS...

HOW TO DRIVE FOR TEN HOURS

Create the right car setup

The car has become your new apartment, and things need to have a spot in which they live, so you don't drive yourself crazy (you're already driving yourself ten hours!):

Lip gloss in center console

Water in cup holder (try to use a reusable water bottle or at least a reusable coffee mug!)

Phone in holder, suctioned to dashboard, charger in phone

Snacks in bag behind passenger seat (not too close)

Sunglasses and regular glasses in backpack on passenger seat

Sunscreen in center console

Baseball cap on passenger seat

Music and podcasts downloaded and ready for quick-clicks

Checklist for car setup does not actually exist on a piece of paper (I'm not that bad)

Let yourself sing

Even if you're not a singer—which I'm not (though I truly believe if I took a few lessons it would be a different story)—singing in the car is one of the last pure joys we have as human beings. In New York apartments, singing straddles a fine line of humiliation. The walls are thin, and you risk being heard. Even though we hardly know our neighbors, and we're comfortable with the brief, friendly encounters in the hallways or on the sidewalk, it's hard to imagine bringing overheard singing into the mix. Cars are the last place we have, our final refuge for belting songs we have no business singing. Ten hours in a car means singing, I'm sorry, it's the truth.

Don't drink too much water, or coffee!

You have to pace yourself because, one, you don't want to have to stop too often, and two, the lack of accessible public bathrooms becomes more and more of a problem the farther you drive into the middle of the country. As much as stopping in new towns and cities might seem fun when planning a road trip, *actually* stopping to use the restroom or find decent coffee in the middle of nowhere (especially off interstates) is...well...shitty. I hate any sort of small-scale confrontation, so I try to avoid having to ask to use the restroom if I'm not buying anything, but the sight of a Starbucks sign on the highway when I've had to pee for two hours completely obliterates any fear of confrontation. Starbucks might be more known for their bathrooms than their coffee.

Be prepared for rain

By prepared, I mean, know it will happen at some point and it will be torrential. Because you're driving for so long, you're bound to drive through rain. It will seem like it came out of nowhere, but in fact, it's *you* who is coming out of nowhere, driving seventy miles an hour (on average) into the rain. But the rain actually isn't the most dangerous part, it's the other people driving in the rain. Some drivers just don't know what to do with weather. That's what the shoulders are for, to lean on if you can no longer operate your vehicle. Hold up, I don't think that's what road or highway engineers were intending, but how adorable is that? Lean on the shoulders when you need them! They're right there to pull off on if you have to catch your breath. The rain and the other people speeding through it can be intense, and your life might briefly flash before your eyes during one of these downpours. But you'll make it through.

Stretching

It didn't occur to me until this trip how my body would feel, sitting in the same position for so many hours at a time. I started putting a roll of paper towels and later a folded-up sweatshirt behind the small of my back to ease the strain. I found interesting ways to stretch my arms while driving and tried using my left foot to operate the car (not recommend) when my right foot would cramp up. In-car stretching is important and should be experimental, like all essential things are.

Jumping up and down

A lot of the smaller rest stops have outdoor areas with picnic tables and overhangs that provide a bit of shade. Hot tip: Bring a towel and free weights and do a quick calisthenics routine outside at these bad boys. I would do jumping jacks, quick reps with three-pound weights, push-ups, and sit-ups. When you're sitting so long you have to get out and jump around for a bit. *SELF* MAGAZINE HERE I COME.

Bring hats

I'm not a huge hat person, other than a few styles I have in my rotation like any sophisticated grown woman does, but on the road, I stuck to a these options:

Baseball cap. You want one of these for the sun. Yeah, you have the front shade in the car that pulls down in front of your face to block the sun, but it'll still creep up on ya. You'll want one of these handy.

Large-brim canvas hat. Cars are the best place to test out hats.

Be bold

The human race is pretty incredible. We've made gigantic leaps in science and technology, in innovation and connectivity. We've created astounding inventions that have changed the whole world. We have sewer systems and fly in the sky from place to place. We FaceTime and Skype like in *The Jetsons*! But when we put our turn signals on and move into the left lane, beginning the bold attempt to pass an eighteen-wheeler, we are truly glorious.

START THE DAY

AUSTIN SHIRT TUCK

I made a deal with myself around the time I turned thirty, years before this last relationship, to try and live my life without needing anyone else. This was around the same time as the *other* deal (I *love* deals), the boldly asking people out situation. *This* deal didn't necessarily negate that one—I'd continue to date and put myself out there, but I started to feel that maybe I shouldn't really *need* anyone else to go after the big mile markers or experiences in life. Maybe I would do them on my own, and that would be all right. It wasn't like a scheduled deal-making meetup (because it was just me), I didn't type out a contract or anything, but there were extensive internal debates, wild objections, and negotiations were ongoing: "Should I buy an apartment on my own? I can actually afford to do it and it makes sense, investment-wise. But maybe I should wait until I'm with someone to create a home together?" "Is it weird to go to Nicaragua for Christmas by myself? Can I really travel alone over the holidays, what will people think?" "It's Saturday night...Do I have to order two sodas so my takeout seems like it's not just for me?" No! Enough of this ridiculousness! I shook my own hand and started the rest of my life with myself anew: I'll go where I want to go, buy what I want with the money I've earned, order whatever takeout I want with disproportionate sodas, do and see what I yearn to experience in the world, even if it means I go alone. If I made those plans for myself without setting any expectation of there being someone beside me, then I could never be disappointed because I was making that choice! This new deal, very similar to Franklin D. Roosevelt's (not similar in any way), had been my mission statement. And this road trip was a renegotiation— I'd veered off course for a while there, and now I was back on track! A single woman, unleashed upon the country—the wind in my hair! But, despite my best intentions, my best negotiation tactics and dealmaking expertise, I found myself in a Pinterest-perfect hotel room in Austin, Texas, not celebrating my independence, but rather still mourning my last relationship. As the T. Rex record I borrowed from the lobby ended (it actually hadn't reached the end of the first side yet, but it's more dramatic if I remember it happening simultaneously), I saw how falling in love had been a deviation from my plan. A lovely, soul-changing detour. I'd ripped up my deal and flung myself into the thing I feared most, someone else. This false armor I'd built around myself to need no one wasn't working, it was only holding me back. I'd have to let it go.

I FaceTimed Ilana. I wanted her to see how beautifully the room was decorated. She was in a taxi, on her way to the airport, about to fly to Europe with her husband. A true vacation. They were so excited. She asked how it was going. I told her this trip was harder than I thought it would be, that I was starting to get sad again. She said, "But you wanted this, right?" I suppose I did. I created this, both the freedom and the loneliness. If we hadn't been on a video chat, the drastic difference I felt in that moment between my life and hers would have shown on my face, but I waited until we hung up to let it fully hit me. I'd never want her to see my sadness in response to her happiness—I felt so proud of her and them. They were so present with each other, so in it, together. But she was right, this *was* my choice, to be alone on this trip, but at the same time what other choice did I have? I don't have a husband or a wife to travel with. If I did, they would have stopped me from eating the entire dish of rosemary Marcona almonds the hotel set out for me! They would have told me I didn't need to buy the fancy crème on display in the bathroom, and they would have surely applied sunscreen to my back before I went down to the pool! But there I was, not only single, but sunburnt and salty.

The next day, I had a dinner plans with a friend, but the rest of my time I had free to wander. I browsed the stores on South Congress and read Sontag essays while I ate brunch at my favorite spot on the corner. I had breakfast there the last time I'd been in Austin, with *her*. I tried to push that out of my mind, to not jump back in time to the last lazy day I explored this neighborhood. I could create new experiences in the same place on my own. Things had changed since I'd been back—new restaurants opened, stores closed, and there seemed to be even more people now, bustling into the air-conditioned shops to get out of the heat. I walked along the sidewalk and caught a glimpse of myself in a store window. Over the past few months,

I'd come to develop a sort of uniform. Maybe it was because it was one less thing to think about, but I'd taken to primarily wearing a long-sleeved shirt or a T-shirt, tucked into jeans. It was a really hot day in Austin, and I was wearing a T-shirt tucked into jean shorts (a new, summer addition to the uniform). I was so different now. I could see it in the reflection.

I realize people have probably been tucking in their shirts since shirts and pants existed, and I am in no way claiming it's my discovery, but I'm stating boldly: In the textbook history of the "shirt tuck," my experience should be noted, studied, and possibly given a pull quote.

I never tucked in my shirts. EVER. I grew up with an extremely stylish mom, who tucked in her shirts and wore cute belts when she did. It just worked on her. My dad tucked in his dress shirts for work every day, without a second thought. I mention my dad here to give equal airtime, but a men's shirt tuck is very different, as I'm sure you know. There's inherent blousing with a button-down, the suit jacket often covers so much. It's a different beast. I'm sure men have a whole other set of insecurities surrounding business attire, how it is for them to tuck in their shirts, what ties are all about and how to keep them from dunking in stuff, etc. That's not my story to tell. But I was around a lot of shirts, tucked into pants. This wasn't new to me. I had been exposed from a young age, but even then, I never wanted anything to do with it. My stomach was chubby and I tended to wear baggy shirts or sweaters so as to not have to deal with feeling insecure about it. A bizarre optical lie I'd quietly convinced myself of, that a loose piece of fabric, draping down past my waist, would blur the reality of what was underneath. I was always fidgeting with my shirts, always trying to cover up some part of myself I thought wasn't good enough to be exposed. Something I wasn't confident enough to show, quietly keeping a distance between the world and my body. I didn't even know I was doing it...just like I didn't know I'd be interested in women.

I remember I was with her one day and we were getting ready to go out to run errands or get dinner. She looked at my outfit and said something like, "You should tuck your shirt in, it would look really good." A silent wave of fear coursed through my body...I don't...do...that. But because it was her, I tried it. She looked at me, smirking, like, *Toldja so.* I smiled, and that was that. And then there was a shift. All of a sudden, I felt more put together, more feminine, more stylish, more confident. It wasn't completely about the shirt, it was also about being with her, I know, but the visible change in the way I carried myself seeped into my body. Life-changing events are usually bigger, more pronounced, and typically don't involve a small adjustment in the way you wear your T-shirts, but this was one for me. I've shown a lot of myself (almost everything) on television, but this was different. It was like tucking in my shirt was me coming out as queer, to myself. I was already with a woman and it was no secret, but this was where I owned it. I claimed it as mine. *This* is who I am and who I want to be. I was proud to be this person, fully. I had never felt more like a woman, more extraordinary, and more in charge.

She knows all this. This shirt-tuck business. It was one of the last things I said to her as we were breaking up. I told her with tears rushing down my face, that she changed my life,

"…you taught me how to tuck in my shirt." What I really meant was she taught me who I was, who I could be if I'd let myself be seen.

I wasn't just in Austin again to go to the same stores or wander around the same neighborhood as last time, even though I did. I came here to track my progress, to see how much I'd changed, to define which mile marker I currently stood at, between her and wherever I was going next. I *was* alone in Austin, but I was alone as a new version of myself, one I could see clearly for once, and damn, that shirt was tucked in beautifully.

NO EXPLANATION
NECESSARY

ON SNACKS

The things we surround ourselves with—how we decorate our homes or office spaces, what we wear and carry around with us—are all clues into who we are and what we care about, what we think about and prioritize. But what about snacks? *What about snacks?* Snacks tell the whole story: our mood, our mind-set, our needs, and our weaknesses. Wow. While driving for hours at a time almost every other day, I've had a chance to do the thinking for all of us regarding snacks. I've curated my own snack inventory for this trip, based on where I'm at currently, physically (also emotionally)—which mostly revolves around the concept of *out of sight, out of body*, which mostly means, if I don't have anything bad in sight it can't end up in my body. I have in my car a bag of snacks that most people would not be excited about. It's functional: nut bars, dried fruit, coffee chews (these intense bite-size chews filled with the caffeine equivalent of a cup of coffee), turkey jerky

(I *am* on a road trip), and a few apples. There's nothing really good—on purpose, I don't want to be snacking the whole trip. But if someone was to come over, into my car or house, I'd change up my whole game, partially to appease what I think they might enjoy, and partially to up my snack style! *Snack Style* is a whole other book, clearly.

Snack style in corporate culture is fascinating—the number of snacks and drinks in Hollywood alone is astounding. While I'm in Los Angeles, I'll be on hiatus from *Broad City*, and will mostly be writing on my own, pitching a few other projects, and taking general meetings (casual networking coffees and conversation). This also means I'll be going to the various networks around town. Even though I have a television show, and I'm technically a part of the industry, Hollywood still remains, for the most part, foreign to me. I operate primarily in New York, which allows me to keep the "business" at a distance. Most of my interaction with the big guns in LA include emails, awkward conference calls, and these occasional in-person pitch meetings. The latter of which, still, without fail, give me a nervous stomach along with the urge to stuff my bag with all the free snacks and drinks, a questionable habit I developed in college. It's hard to not take the free stuff! I could write a whole piece detailing the character of each network I've been to through the snacks and overall ambience they provide in their lobby and kitchen areas. A testament to my new, revised theory of how everything we are is in everything we do, even when it comes to snacks. You know what, I *will* do that, as it's something the world has clearly been waiting to hear. The thing in Hollywood that needs to be exposed, *finally*.

COMEDY CENTRAL: Pictures of me everywhere, and…it's incredible! I kid, but I'm biased with this one, so I can't include them in my important and highly anticipated exposé. There *are* photos of me though, and every single time I walk in, my mind is blown.

NETFLIX: The lobby is fun and fresh, but a tad overwhelming. There's a lot going on, in drastically different ways, perhaps akin to their…programming? Huge screens occupy major wall space, all playing different content. New shows! Huge stars! Movie trailers! Animation! These screens are Netflix's hype men, getting you pumped to enter through the turnstiles, and it works. Another wall is completely covered in lush plants—those weird, in-the-wall plant designs you only see in super-hipster coffee shops. I went on a deep dive once, googling these wall plants, searching for the how and why of it all. Did I think I was going to install one in my New York City apartment? The watering requirements alone are far beyond my capabilities. I struggle to keep the one and a half plants I already own alive. I sometimes forget to take myself to the doctor! I can't take on this type of responsibility. Also, I bet if you have one of these wall plants, it suddenly becomes the most significant thing about you. It's probably all people want to talk about, and I have other things I want to talk about. I made the right decision and came away satisfied in the knowledge that some things are just out of my reach. Moving along into the Netflix kitchen(s)—they have *everything*. All the legit LA stuff: top brands of kombucha, coconut water, the concentrated iced coffee in the little glass bottles (you have to be careful with these, there's a reason CONCENTRATED is printed in large font), fruit! They even have branded candies for their shows. I slipped a *Stranger Things* sucker into my pocket when no one was looking. They want you to be a fan, to geek out.

HBO: Nothing. It is a huge, sterile lobby. You know immediately you are supposed to be quiet in here, there's an unspoken seriousness. There's some sort of huge sculpture hanging from the ceiling or on the floor in the middle of the room (I didn't dare get too up close), a jarring, glowing orb. It's probably just an "artful" light fixture, but it gives off a metallic, cold presence. It sounds as though I critique all light fixtures this thoughtfully, like some sort of lamp sommelier. I don't usually, but this one was definitely NOT fruity, but *did* leave a strong aftertaste. There is nothing in the lobby (food- or drinks-wise) and no one asks you if you want anything. You're lucky if there's water on the conference table when you get inside. This says everything. This is the place that doesn't need to sell anyone. The place that expects to be sold *to*. I'm not even knocking it. It's working for them. They have curated a space to hold the upper hand.

HULU: The lobby is small, covered in hundreds of framed photos of people and projects they are in some way involved with, like a cozy power-wall. There's hardly any seating, so if there's more than one group waiting for a meeting, you might end up awkwardly standing around trying not to knock a photo off the wall. I'm not sure if this was their intention, but an abundance of framed photos and a lack of ample seating can lead to a low-key power move...well played, Hulu, well played. The group I was with got into the kitchen (which is more for employees only here), insisting that we could grab coffee ourselves. This kitchen is *stocked*. They have those cereal dispensers, the ones with the levers at the bottom, a staple in every college dining hall. Always filled with all the best, nostalgic brands, including what appeared to be KASHI GOOD FRIENDS cardboard nonsense. I used to hang with GOOD FRIENDS back in the day when cereal was good for you. I circled the machine...I wasn't going to bring a bowl of cereal into the pitch meeting—I'm not a maniac! But I thought about it. I thought about it for a long while. THEN, *inside* the conference room they have baskets of snacks. It's like a spread of "healthy" snack food from the '90s, you know, the low-fat health bars and fruit snacks like Nature Valley, SnackWell's, etc. Not my cup of tea, but nonetheless, Hulu does go all out. Not sure exactly who they are just yet, they try to please everyone.

AMAZON: I feel like I might have had to sign a non-disclosure agreement to even enter the parking garage here, so I'm going to be careful. They have a little, unassuming serve-yourself coffee cart in the lobby and an even littler bowl of candy at the desk where you sign away your first child. I was pleasantly surprised at the abundance of pink and red Starburst. Either people are opting for the other flavors, which doesn't make *any* sense at all, or they've somehow managed to only purchase pinks and reds. To actually enter the space where the meetings are held, you have to wear a keycard around your neck and be escorted inside what seems to be a bulletproof doorway. You are instructed to never remove this keycard while "inside," and when you leave, your first thought *must* be to return the keycard. The keycard is more important than the pitch meeting! Not sure exactly what they're hiding in there, but clearly, their secrets start with the pink and red Starburst.

FX: I don't think there is a lobby here, or a kitchen? The walls are lined with posters of their content, not unlike other networks, but here, there's no space to wait or sit. The lack of hospitality makes us weaklings want to be here even more, want to prove ourselves. Pshh, you know what, I don't need a place to sit! I love standing! I don't care if you've passed on all the shows I've ever brought to you! I have my dignity, I could stand here forever! Is this one getting too personal?

NETWORK: I've only been to NBC, ABC, FOX, and CBS a handful of times. I'm lumping them together because I honestly can't pinpoint any real difference in their lobby experiences. They're very corporate, and they don't really make an effort to design their spaces (or snacks) in any way that reveals their identity. Or maybe, they're doing exactly that. Every time I go into one of these offices I know in my gut it's just not right. Me pitching to a network is probably my one opportunity in life to be the bad girl on a motorcycle (obviously sans helmet) taking the girl next door out on a date. We both know it's wrong, that it's not gonna work out between us. Sure, maybe she'd wanna fuck me, to make sure it's not the right match, to cover her bases and have no regrets. But the sex would just be okay, because I did it her way and didn't get to fully express all my sexual prowess as a motorcycle-riding-wild-woman, didn't get to explore why this sex needed to be had at this particular point in time, or make the sex actually funny! By the time she was done with me, she'd have developed that script into the ground. Sorry, sex. Sorry, snacks.

FOR OLD TIMES' SAKE

WHEN IN AUSTIN

WHITTINGTON'S

TURKEY
JERKY

SALTY "SNACK STYLE"

THERE WAS A POINT IN TIME WHEN
ILANA + I ORDERED THIS IN BULK.

... IT WAS AN INTERESTING TIME

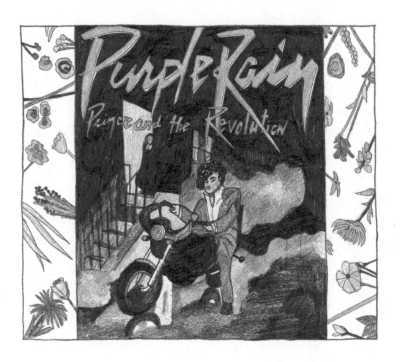

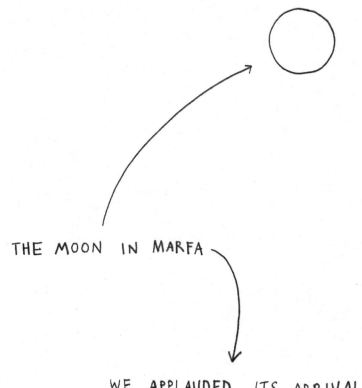

THE MOON IN MARFA

WE APPLAUDED ITS ARRIVAL

MARFA SLEEP STUDY

Alarm set on phone: 7:00 a.m.
Do Not Disturb: on
Brainwaves App: Set to—OCEAN WAVES 2—for 1 hour
Lights: off

11:36 p.m.

That was a fun night. I was nervous to be with these new people, on my own, but it was really special. They were so kind to me. Lately I've been feeling distrustful of new people, and I'd forgotten what it was like to make new friends. It's so much harder now to really connect and feel like there's a possibility of longevity there. It's nice to know I can still do it, that there are new people out there who will become part of my life.

I wonder if I could just pick up and move to a random city where I knew no one, and begin again? I think I could. I guess anyone could. I don't want to, but it's nice to know I could. I could be okay.

11:51 p.m.

I've never slept in an Airstream before, it's so cozy. I wonder how much these things cost? I guess this one would have to be towed. Then you gotta get like a huge pickup truck to drive it around. I could live in here for a while, for sure. This is a high-end version though—who wouldn't be able to live in here? It's beautiful. It wouldn't be so different from the whole "van life" situation. There's a whole new wave of people driving around the country living in vans, instagramming. That seems to come around every few years, the whole "van life" thing. I guess it's good for the van manufacturers?

What happened to Van Morrison? Is he still alive? Great voice. I should pull him up tomorrow on the drive. "Glad Tidings." That song. I have to pull that up right when I'm driving into some insane landscape tomorrow. I'll remember. Was he the one who changed his name? No, that's Cat Stevens. Why do I always put those two together? Maybe because I had those CDs next to one another in my CD book.

Ohh man, Dave Jensen's CD book. That was so bad. What even happened? We went to get a bite, and on our way back to his house, he realized his huge CD case wasn't in the car anymore, it had somehow fallen out when we went into the restaurant or to the gas station? We backtracked and looked in all those parking lots—nothing. I felt terrible. He was so bummed. *Dave.* We were stoned and stupid. I was always stoned and doing idiotic things in high school. I wonder who found his CDs—a huge CD carrying case full of Steve Miller Band and classic rock. I hope it ended up with someone who was thrilled to find it. All his music. "The Joker," that song always makes me think of him.

I'm going to play that tomorrow. If I think about him, it makes it like he's still around.

12:13 a.m.

Shit! These bugs. I cannot believe how bit up I am from being outside tonight. My legs are covered. These bites are gonna keep me up all night. I have to remember to use the bug spray I bought.

Marfa is so cute. There's one general store everyone goes to. It must be nice to have less options. I feel overwhelmed with options. I guess that's not such a bad thing. I love how quiet it is here. The pace is slower. I couldn't even find coffee after 3 p.m. today! Marfa is exposing my coffee addiction in a big way.

12:26 a.m.

You actually *shouldn't* be able to get whatever you want at ALL times. That's the problem with New York—when you leave, you expect everywhere to be operating on the same time line, the same infrastructure, and that's not how it should be. It's like I just go around thinking I should be able to get coffee whenever I damn well please! What an asshole. When the apocalypse happens I won't be able to do anything on my own because I'm used to being able to get anything I want or need at any time.

Stop thinking about the apocalypse.

I have to remember to get those supplies. The straws and batteries and stuff for the go bag. I gotta write that down.

12:40 a.m.

I'll be totally on my own if something ever happened. Will I be able to find new friends during an apocalypse? I guess they'd be more like allies? This is a reason to wear sneakers more often. Imagine if the end of the world happened and I was wearing heels?! That would be the worst—I wouldn't make it. I don't think my bare feet would adapt fast enough. I'd probably have to make shoes—I think I would actually be good at that, fashioning shoes and clothes in an apocalyptic situation. But wearing sneakers from the onset would prolong the chances of survival for sure. I should keep a pair in my car. For other reasons too—like if I want to go on a hike or if my shoes are hurting me...but also to be the shoes that might save my life...or the last shoes I'll ever wear. Stop this!

1:02 a.m.

I won't know anyone for the rest of the trip. It'll be okay. I need this space.

Maybe I won't talk to anyone, make a thing of it, a code of silence for the rest of the trip. I could figure out a way to do that with hotel employees, to check in and out without talking. Those silent retreats always seemed interesting. I guess I'll feel it out.

1:18 a.m.

Go to sleep right now. Just. Go. To. Sleep.

Focus on your breath.

Damn the waves stopped. I'm not even going to restart them, this is a fake thing.

1:21 a.m.

Everyone has dogs here. It was nice to be around a little pack. Ugh, I want a dog so badly. I know that was just a terrible time for me and didn't really have anything to do with the dog, but now I'm just scared I'll fuck it up again. Maybe I'm so selfish I can't take care of anything but myself. Not only can I not be in a relationship, I can't even have a dog in my life.

What a piece of shit.

1:30 a.m.

Don't think like that.
Don't think like that.
Don't think like that.

I have to go outside.

1:49 a.m.

Okay. I'm going to sleep right now. Then I'm gonna wake up and get in the car and drive to Santa Fe.

I'm not a piece of shit. If I think that about myself then what am I even doing here. I'm on this trip to try and feel better, not make myself feel worse. I have to have my own back. Okay then.

Here we go. Go to sleep you fuckface.

Haha.

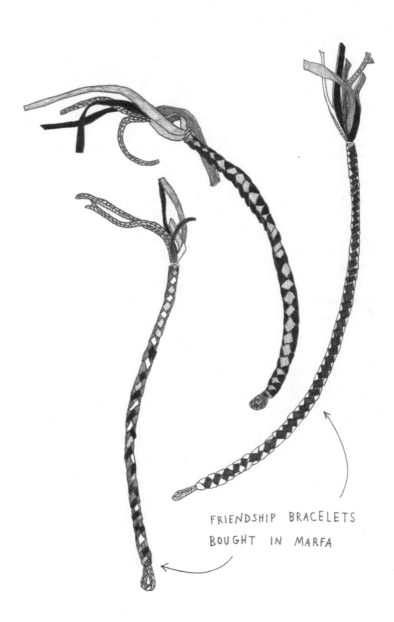

FRIENDSHIP BRACELETS
BOUGHT IN MARFA

Petrichor

| ˈpeˌtrīkôr |

Noun

A pleasant smell that frequently accompanies the first rain after a long period of warm, dry weather.

Other than the petrichor emanating from the rapidly drying grass, there was not a trace of evidence that it had rained at all.

NEW APP

MINOR REGRETS

As I drove past antiques markets and dozens of peach farms, I started thinking about the small things I wished I'd done (like stopping for a peach). Ways in which I'd handled situations in the past and actions I full-on regret. There are so many deeper regrets, so many things I didn't say to people who aren't around anymore, things I did say. Moments I don't like to even think about because they're too painful. But these smaller missteps are just as important. Living without regrets is impossible, but for me keeping them in a mental file, tucked away, safe and sound, can come in handy. I can go through them once in a while to see how much I've grown, see the old versions of myself, lined up next to one another, knowing that this version of me, right now, will soon join the pack.

Elijah Wood

In fourth grade, I concocted an elaborate scheme to convince my elementary school bus-mates that Elijah Wood was my cousin. I'm not sure why I did this, or why I'd decided to make him related to me, as my only real connection with him was thinking he was adorable, cutting out *Bop* magazine clippings of him, and hanging them on my wall next to Will Smith and Jonathan Brandis. This isn't really that terrible of a crime, and I'm not even sure if I completely regret it, but the deceit feels worth mentioning. I brought in a framed photo of a young Elijah Wood (no doubt snipped from another *Bop* or *Big Bopper* magazine), and put an even younger photo of my actual cousin Cory, who only shares brown hair with Sir Wood, behind it, to prove somehow that we'd been updating his photos as he aged? The frame alone was the key to the whole ploy. When you put a photo inside a frame, it changes everything, it becomes real and has meaning. My bus-mates bought it! I succeeded in lying about being related to a young actor known best for his popular roles in *The Good Son* and *North*. Great? There was no endgame except the satisfaction of being able to create a story and execute it well enough to make it seem real. I'm finding a bunch of my regrets, innocent as they may be, revolved around me creating things other people believed that I then felt bad about. I suppose I was bound to become a writer. A writer or an actor. A writer or an actor or a con man.

Jewish genes

I grew up in a town that wasn't very Jewish at all. I was probably one of ten Jewish kids in my school, and my only Jewish friends were from camps I went to over the summer. I wasn't very religious, but did go to Sunday school and even had a Bat Mitzvah. I could read Hebrew, but was never taught what I was reading, so looking back, my Jewish education feels half-assed. I could read words out loud but not understand them? Why didn't we learn the other half of knowing a language? Years of Wednesday evening and Sunday morning classes, done for one night of performance art (my Bat Mitzvah), where I stood on the altar and competed with my frizzy hair for the leading role. There was a girl in my school who was also Jewish, but she didn't have a Bat Mitzvah, and I remember questioning her about if she was in fact Jewish if she didn't have this ceremony? The ceremony I just mentioned as having no real stake in, one where I could have been reciting a Hebrew dictionary for all I knew. What a dick. I don't know if I really meant it in that tone, but I had no clue what Jewish meant or was, and I sure as hell wasn't evolved enough to understand that there are varying degrees of religion and beliefs for everyone. I know that she probably questioned her Judaism because of me, and I've always felt a lot of guilt about it. Maybe I'm more Jewish than I think?

Hot-wire

I hot-wired a car and was the getaway driver for a bank robbery in 1998. This is a lie, but wouldn't that be incredible!? What if I was Baby Driver?! While I'm here I want to mention the fact that I think that movie, *Baby Driver*, would have been *way better* if the role of Baby was a woman (or if any woman in the movie said more words than a baby might). I think this about almost all films, as most of the nuanced, fun, and risky characters are men. Would you believe it less if it was a woman? Right, only a straight white guy with floppy hair can play a highly skilled getaway driver with an inner-ear problem and bizarre social skills. The film would completely lose its relatability if it was a woman! How would we pay attention!? How would we laugh at that!? While I'm inside this room, getting down and dirty—I woulda KILLED it as Baby! Come on, you'd watch that movie! Me sitting in a getaway car, scrolling the wheel of the original iPod, searching for the perfect song to drive away to. Oh, man, that would have been something special. You can put your bookmark in here now if you need a second to process, no pressure to continue right into the next minor regret. That was a lot to take in.

"Little Suzie"

I went to overnight camp for a very long time—twelve years. I started at ten years old and was a camper until I was sixteen. And *then* I was a counselor until I was twenty-one. There's a lot to be said about this experience, but this is about one tiny thing I remember from when I was about twelve. One day that summer I made up this song, "Little Suzie"—the only lyrics being: "I went to the market, to see my little Suzie. When I got there, she wasn't there, so I left her allllooooooooone." It's the type of song that doesn't really jump off the page, one where the performance plays a significant role. Anyways, I was singing this song and ended up asking a few of my bunkmates if they'd heard it. One of them said, "Yeah, of course I know that song!" I proceeded to say, "Ohh, do you?! *'Cause I just made it up!?*" Again…what a dick! I particularly don't like when people pretend to know things they don't, and strongly believe it's okay to NOT know everything. It's all right to not know every song and it doesn't make you uncool. So, part of me was like—why are you doing that, annoyed that she felt the need to fake it, but looking back now with my adult glasses on, I see she was just trying to fit in and I called her out, in fact I set her up. NOT COOL, ABBI, not cool at all. There's so much content to consume, a constant flow of news stories and one scandal after the other to keep track of. It would be crazy to know everything let alone every piece of pop culture. That's why we have friends and co-workers, family and interactions with people at all, so we can share what we know with them and vice versa. So, yeah, I was a huge asshole about my hit song, but "Little Suzie" and its catchy chorus always reminds me to be a bit kinder in this world of overflowing information.

Fixing the raffle

When I was about seven and my brother was ten or eleven, I fixed a raffle at our elementary school so that he and his girlfriend at the time, Whitney Star, would win. I was selected, I'm not sure how or why, to be the one to put her hand into a bowl of crumpled pieces of paper with names written on them and pick the winner. I came up with a scheme, completely on my own, to write their names (Brian Jacobson and Whitney Star), each on a separate piece of paper, and already have them in my tiny hand when I put it into the bowl. So then, when I removed it, I'd have selected their names! Lots of questions and concerns here: Where would I have seen something like this? Why I was willing to risk life and limb so that my brother and his girlfriend would win this raffle? When did my childhood turn into a B-story from an episode of Full House? This holiday extravaganza was held in the cafeteria with booths selling crafts and baked goods. There were a lot of people in attendance and the drawing of the winners was an anticipated event. Everyone had stopped doing what they were doing to see who won. Me drawing my own brother's name was highly unlikely, and when I did, it clearly meant I had fixed the raffle! On top of that, I was only supposed to draw one name! What was I thinking!? But I was seven and extremely scrappy, if I do say so myself. This is an adorable way to cheat the system. The whole room, including my parents and my brother and Whitney Star, immediately knew what I'd done. But all in all, a slick way to do it, right? Pretty clever for a seven-year-old. I don't know if I actually regret this one, I like this kid.

Hotel bathroom

I wish I'd had sex this one night with this guy in a hotel bathroom. I was hooking up with him after a Bar Mitzvah for which I'd been hired by the family to take photos. I'm not sure how I fell into this, but there was a brief period of time during college where I was being hired by friends or friends of my dad's to take photos at events for a couple hundred bucks. That was a ton of money for me at the time especially since I was using a terrible digital camera. I'm not talking about a high-end digital camera, I'm referring to those tiny digital cameras where you slide the piece of plastic over to expose the lenses. The ones where you have no control over anything—total point and shoot. Did I also mention I'm not a photographer? I fear these photos, capturing important milestones like Bar and Bat Mitzvahs and high school reunions, were not in the best hands. I suppose they got their $200 worth, but I'm now consumed with a larger fear that one of these people will read this, go back and look at said photos, and realize how awful they are. How that moment in their child's life wasn't properly captured, how people's faces are probably cut off and everyone's eyes are red. How me not being able to figure out the right flash setting might not have set the scene properly. If that is you in this moment then, listen, memories are *way* more important than photos, and that's the real takeaway here. Maybe I did you a favor? So, on this particular night, I was taking photos at a Bar Mitzvah of a family I went to camp with. I had hooked up with this guy the previous summer and we now found ourselves in our mutual friend's hotel room, making out in the bathroom. I don't know why I didn't have sex with him, it was a clear mis-handling of the situation. I had two hundred bucks in my bag, hazy circles in my eyes from the terrible flash, and my priorities weren't lined up. I should have fucked that extremely hot, sweet guy on the toilet of that hotel bathroom and I didn't.

Two onions

My first year in New York, I interned in the art department of the Onion News Network. I tried my best to make friends with my "boss" but she was just terrible to me. I was so excited about the job—to potentially blend my artistic skill set with my new love of comedy—but she didn't want any of it, and I'm not even sure why I was hired. It was such a short time, maybe a month and a half, but this was 2006 and if I still remember these two incidents, then they're significant to me. Time doesn't dictate impact. Not that this moment was major, I will just never forget it. We were shooting a sketch in a hospital all the way uptown in Manhattan and it was a long day. I was carrying a bunch of garments on hangers, and I had to go bring them back to where we were storing everything—a room they'd given us on a lower floor. I got in the elevator with this boss—who I should say was maybe a year or two older than me. I went to push the button for this lower floor, and she Slapped. My. Hand. She actually slapped my hand! She then pressed another floor and reprimanded me in front of a bunch of other people who were also working on the show...because I pressed the wrong floor!? Bright Lights Big City, I had entered Hollywood, ladies and gentlemen! Was everyone a complete shithead? I should also point out, I had pressed the right floor and someone else corrected her. I regret not quitting, right then and there. It's hard to stand up for yourself when you're new and young and scared.

I did quit the next week though. I sat across a desk from the woman who was my boss's boss and began to tell her I was done. Thank you, but I didn't like working there, it wasn't right for me. She then proceeded to somehow convince me to go to *her* boss's apartment and set up his DVD player. WHAT THE ACTUAL FUCK?? And then…I did it?! Abbi! Abbi Lee Jacobson! I had just quit, because I felt terrible in this environment. It made me question working in comedy for fear that this was how everyone was, and then I bashfully went to this apartment and unsuccessfully tried to set up this dude's DVD player. Ugh. I wish I could hug my younger self and take her out for a nice dinner. Tell her that this is hilarious and is okay. We all do things because we're scared and intimidated. Last week, eleven years later, I sold a TV show with the dude whose DVD player I unsuccessfully set up. Welcome to Hollywood, baby!

Hooking up with girls

I regret not having hooked up with or dated girls in college. What a major missed opportunity. I don't really remember being into anyone, women-wise, at that point in my life, and I like to think I would have acted on it if I was, but art school feels like a place where that would have been fun. I was so shy there, so extremely introverted. So different than the versions of my-self that bookend those four years. But I should have fucked at least one girl, right?

Not going on a raid at camp

I wish I'd gone on a raid when I was ten. For those of you who didn't go to overnight camp for twelve years and have no idea what a raid is, I'll fill you in. A raid is when you sneak out of your bunk in the middle of the night, usually to a bunk of the opposite sex. As you get older it can include a wide range of sexual encounters, different forms of smoking, etc. Sometimes just talking! WILD! [Note: I went on raids as I got older—both the sexual and talking variety.] But I was ten and it was my first year at overnight camp, and I hated it. I was terribly homesick, and it's hard to believe I ever went back, let alone for eleven more summers. On this night, my entire bunk was go-ing on a raid to the boys' bunk, and I decided not to. I was so nervous and hadn't really found my place among the other girls yet. I just couldn't bear the thought of getting in trouble. I wish as a kid I was less afraid of getting caught. I wish I took more risks, but I didn't. My whole bunk went on the raid as I lay in my tiny bed, under the covers, wishing I'd gone. They all got caught and were docked, meaning they couldn't go to the dance that next Sunday night. But I wasn't docked, so I went to the dance. This was just the fucking worst. Ten-year-old me, not comfortable in my own skin or clothes or hair, stood alone be-cause I didn't muster the courage to do something outside the box. I went back to the bunk and hung out with my friends. It was the first time I realized that the rules aren't always meant to be followed. You're supposed to break them sometimes, especially if you want to experience the best stuff.

Venison Boy

When I was a freshman in college there was this boy, this senior that I had a crush on. He lived in a town house a few streets away from my dorm and I don't even know how we first met, but I know that we flirted from the outset, chatting a bit here and there, smiling from afar on our way to classes. He had a beard and was a sculpture major or something really sexy like that where he worked with his hands. I was enamored. I'd walk down his street on my way home to my dorm, hoping to run into him. Then, one day, he invited me over for dinner the following night... to his house!? Something I'd wanted to happen for weeks was goin' down and could it be true that I had made it happen? When I arrived, in a cute outfit for the time, which would be a terrible outfit now, I saw that it was him and his roommates having dinner. I was bummed, and thought it was going to be more intimate, but I ran with it, making small talk with his roommates, trying to be cool enough to hang with other seniors. They'd been grilling stuff on the back patio for dinner and I didn't question what it was, but then it was announced that dinner was ready. We sat down at the table and I found out: Dinner was *venison*. They'd gotten a deer somehow from someone, or a big piece of one, and were cooking it…They all acted like this was a casual, normal thing, and I became quiet, and withdrew into my freshman, non-meat-eating body. I don't eat meat, at least not game-y meat like venison. I've never had a hamburger and I know you're like, "Excuse me?" as that seems to be a detail people latch onto. Anyways, I've never had a hamburger and haven't eaten beef since I was twelve. But I ate this fucking venison. Or at least a little piece of it. I did so for this guy, and for what? I'll tell you what—to be informed late in the evening all about his fucking girlfriend!? What are we doing here?? How could he not know why I was there, that I was eating deer for *him*!? I ate deer for this bearded fuck and he has a girlfriend? This is a story like many stories in my life where unfortunately, I was living on a completely different plane of reality than the person in front of me. Basically, I had been invited over there because they had a pile of deer meat, and they needed more stomachs to store it. BULLSHIT, buddy! And guess what, Venison Boy—I don't even know your name. I didn't even pretend to know it or try to come up with a fake one. I regret eating that meat for that boy whose name has left me.

BAT CAVES

Carlsbad Caverns
National Park

Park Entrance   0.2 mi.
Visitor Center   6.8 mi.

VISITOR CENTER OPEN
8:00 — 7:00
MOUNTAIN TIME

I GOT TOO NERVOUS + KEPT DRIVING

SANTA FE BACKLOT

I drove into Santa Fe during magic hour, that transient period of time in between day and night, when the light is just perfect. I checked in, and hurried through the hallways of my hotel, lugging my bags to my room as quickly as possible with the hope I might be able to get back outside and find a spot for dinner before the sun completely set. Once outside, I skipped the first few restaurants I passed near my hotel, as they seemed too obvious—the busy spots right on the square, bustling with tourists—I was a tourist, but not *that* kind of tourist. I needed to find the hole-in-the-wall, the hidden gem. After checking out the one place I'd been recommended by a new friend I met in Marfa and leaving upon realizing I would be seated at a large, round communal table (I have to really be in the mood for that), I was ready to eat almost anywhere. I had pretty much given up on whatever invisible standard I'd seemed to be holding myself to when I stumbled upon a tiny Mexican restaurant with outdoor seating in the middle of an alley. This was the kind of spot I was looking for! It wasn't fancy, not even particularly cute, but it was busy enough that I could believe the food would be decent and I liked the fact that they put their outdoor seating in the middle of an alleyway that still had cars slowly maneuvering around it. That's a bold move, and I love an outdoor seating area with chutzpah. I read Joan Didion (cliché, I am aware) over fajitas for two (touché, my *own* cliché) and watched the sun finish its descent. The next day I wandered around the main square past other tourists and dipped in and out of shops devoted entirely to turquoise bracelets. It's astonishing how I spent two days in Santa Fe and didn't leave completely covered in turquoise.

Santa Fe was so different than anywhere I'd ever been, a quaint, small town full of Native American art and history. The pace felt distinct and significant, but as much as I was enjoying the vibe, I couldn't seem to get away from a nagging thought. I didn't want to acknowledge it, because I felt terrible, but it kept returning: "This place...looks fake?"

I pushed it out of my head, "It's not fake, I'm here, this is a beautiful, real city!" I circled blocks, took photos of adobe rooftops and artisans' knickknacks in outdoor markets. I studied the architecture, the color, the way the tops of buildings seemed to slope randomly with asymmetrical curves, subtly breaking all the rules. Then, it came to me, I knew what it was. Santa Fe felt like a studio backlot in Los Angeles. I know this is an insulting description of an extremely charming city, and I apologize to the people of Santa Fe for my limited cultural knowledge and my annoying habit of comparing one place to another. Maybe it was the light, or the abundance of tourists? Or maybe I've become so Hollywood, I can no longer experience actual culture? I don't even spend time on LA backlots, I've only ever driven through them, hanging off some executive's golf cart, and that was probably because the executive felt bad for not buying the show I was there to pitch them in the first place. I guess that's the problem with working in the business of making fake things seem real—when you see the actual, *real* thing, you can't always appreciate it. Kudos to the backlot designers though, you're clearly killing it.

It's a wild privilege to govern a made-up universe and design lives and a tone. It's thrilling and empowering to write characters and decide how they'll grow, fail, spiral, who they fuck, even when they slip and fall (which my character does quite often). But more and more, it's become a mirror, reflecting the difference in my own life: the planned and executed process of a television show versus the sprawling, unknown storyline of an effortlessly ravishing, ultra-sophisticated, thirty-three-year-old woman.

Lately, *Broad City* has begun to permeate into my whole being. It's become a visual diagram of sorts in which I track my own life, where I've been and where I'm going. The show is the thing that has defined me thus far professionally, the thing all future endeavors will probably be compared with. But it is a *reproduction* of my reality. An exaggerated reproduction, obviously, but one in which the core of *Abbi and Ilana*, and the DNA of the New York City we created within the show, is a copy of us, a "ditto" of the city we inhabited in our twenties. Reproducing something so close to my own experience has forced me to pay close attention, to be more aware of the changes occurring both within the show and within myself. The show had become so familiar, and safe, that I couldn't help but worry—like Mike Teavee in *Willy Wonka*, if we get sucked into the fake world on the screen for too long, we might get stuck.

Ilana and I had recently decided that we would end the show after the fifth season. We'd been debating what felt right for us and, more important, what felt right for *them*, the other Abbi and Ilana. Shows shouldn't go on forever, the best end before they've outstayed their welcome, and in editing Season 4, I had been feeling a strong pull. It's so extremely rare to have the ability to make that decision to end on our own terms. It's a gift and a real testament to Comedy Central and their support of the content that they've let us make that call. What a bizarre turn of events. To have your wildest dreams come true, and then to begin the conversation on when and how that particular dream should end.

To contemplate the end, I have to go back to the beginning:

I met Ilana in an improv practice group in 2007. It was at a shitty rehearsal space in Midtown, one of many, rented out by the hour to practice the art of improv. It sounds counterintuitive to practice improvising, but it was, at least for me, about learning to unlearn. Improv and the core beliefs behind it were like a bible of values I didn't know I was looking for: Don't think. Yes, and. Support. Always have each other's backs. Use the top of your intelligence. It was invigorating and it also scared the shit out of me. I don't think I'd ever, in my whole life, purposely put myself in a more terrifying situation than getting up on stage and doing improv. But it was the rawest, most incredible high I'd ever felt. The things we are most afraid of are the things that will ultimately change our whole makeup.

I found improv on a fluke. It was September of 2006, and I'd been in New York City for a little over a month, living in Astoria, Queens. I moved to the city because I'd been accepted to the Atlantic Theatre Conservatory, a two-year acting program. I was set on being a serious actor, and I aimed for the tippity-top of the seriousness shelf, Mamet, baby! I attended classes for one week and lost my shit—I couldn't do it, I wasn't good enough. I broke down on the northeast corner of 15th Street and Eighth Avenue and I think of that moment every single time I see someone cry in public. Crying publicly is a rite of passage in New York. A rite of passage, a weekly activity, whatever you want to call it. I was twenty-two and had no idea what I was going to do next. I was the first person in my entire family to move outside of the Philadelphia area, for a career that couldn't be more foreign or unrealistic to anyone I'd ever met. I'm sure Atlantic is wonderful for a lot of students. I'm sure they've left feeling inspired and changed and legitimate dramatic actors. But the classes made me paralyzed, trapped inside my own head, unable to speak—the dissection of dialogue and the repetition left me with the constant feeling I was doing it all wrong. It isn't how my brain works. I know that now, but at the time, I felt like a complete failure. I had to make a decision fast or I would lose my initial deposit. Should I stay and stick it out even though my body seemed to be having an allergic reaction to every part of this place, or quit? I quit. I had moved to New York City for this opportunity, and almost immediately, quit. I felt immature, adrift, and like a fraud. I'd repeat that in my head for weeks afterward, silently insulting, scolding, and tearing myself down—I suppose the repetition class wasn't completely lost on me! It's comforting now to reflect on these moments, the pivotal mistakes, the forks in the road. To look back and know it's okay, it was all part of it. The comfort lies really in my future self, eventually looking back at me now in this current, heartbroken state, thinking—*It's okay, it was all part of it.*

At the time of the great "Quickly Quitting My Dreams" movement of 2006, I had a day job as a sales associate at the Anthropologie at Rockefeller Center—something I was excited to share with my character in Season 4 of *Broad City*. I did, like *Abbi* says on the show, grow up in Wayne, Pennsylvania, the town where Anthropologie built their first brick-and-mortar store, so there was a weird, suburban familiarity in working there. But more than that, I'd specifically sought out the Rockefeller location for its proximity to *Saturday Night Live*. It was the closest I could get. I *basically* worked at *SNL*...or rather, counted windows up to the eighth floor and stared longingly from the street. I *loved SNL*. I grew up watching the old reruns on Comedy Central, went as characters for Halloween, and even made a bet with my brother that by the time I was twenty, I'd become a cast member (I still owe him that hundred bucks). Growing up I was hardly involved in school plays, as they were mostly musicals, but I did perform many incarnations of *SNL* sketches—the Cheerleaders, Mary Katherine Gallagher, and Roseanne Roseannadanna—at sleepovers and before basketball or soccer practice, and anywhere else I could find an audience. In eighth grade, I was my homeroom's student council representative, and instead of just reporting the monthly issues I'd seen at the student council meetings back to my homeroom, I reported them *as* Linda Richman (the Mike Myers character), doing *Coffee Talk*. Around this time, I wrote Lorne Michaels a letter telling him to watch out for me, because I'd be there one day. I think I even wrote that he should save the letter, that he'd see! This letter was either never read, dumped in the trash, or flagged as threatening? "*Watch out for me*!?" What balls. So, getting out of the subway and walking past Rockefeller Center on my way to work was a thrill to say the least.

One night around this time, I came home after work, still bummed about my acting fail, and my roommate, a friend I'd gone to college with, brought up this place, the Upright Citizens Brigade. I did a lot of characters in my video work at school and she recommended I go see a show, thinking I would really respond to it. I had never heard of it, or the television show with the same name (I clearly hadn't branched out from *SNL*), but, without much else on my plate, I checked it out. I went alone and having not really seen much live comedy I had no idea what to expect. I found a seat in the back and watched a show, about what I couldn't say, but I sat there in complete awe, paralyzed in a new way. *This.* This thing, whatever unexplainable thing they were doing on that stage, I wanted in. It was astounding, this group of people got up there and were wild and reckless and then somehow pulled it all together to make complete sense. I laughed in more ways at weirder things than I knew were possible. I had stumbled into a basement under a Gristedes and found exactly what I needed. That roommate and I don't speak anymore. She and her boyfriend were the seed of inspiration for my character's living situation on *Broad City*. We hadn't spoken for years by the time the show was on the air, though I'm sure me exaggerating that experience on television probably sealed the deal. That said, my comedy career can be traced back to that frustrating evening after work, her thoughtfully pointing me in my next direction. I will forever be grateful to her for that recommendation, and also for those tumultuous months when her boyfriend moved in to our apartment and ate some of my food.

I started taking classes at UCB as soon as I could, and even though I was scared almost constantly, it was a different fear than at Atlantic. The energy at UCB was smart and quick and alive. I was still timid, but I stayed, knowing if I paid attention and threw myself into this, I could one day do the thing I realized I wanted, to make people laugh. Improvising was such a mix of emotions: like you've taken a drug and discovered a new color, and also like you might have the shits at any moment, right in the middle of the room. I had never participated in something I was so enamored with, or whose tricks and secrets I was so eager to learn. I'd go to see as many live shows as I could, studied my favorite players' styles, read books about technique. There was even an improv resource center online (the IRC), a site run by the community, full of comments and theories. I would read it all, take in as much as I could. I had found my tribe. I didn't yet have the courage or confidence to walk among them; instead, I trailed behind until I did, like a kid sister not fully integrated in the fun outing.

Improv, and long-form improv specifically, is often compared to a cult, because its followers succumb to its teachings, willing to sacrifice all other personal socializing, shedding all extra income on classes and practices, performance spaces and coaches. And it is, if you love it; you get sucked into that high, as a performer and an audience member. It takes over. There were no whisperings of buying land in Oregon just yet, but UCB would go on to open up more locations, so who knows. When I was a student, I remember reading something Amy Poehler (who is one of the four founders of the UCB) wrote about improv, that it was her church, her religion. I felt that way. It was a meeting place, a gathering full of people trying their best to expand themselves and learn. The ultimate goal was to be present, and to laugh, together. In everyday life, the chance for that sort of connection and collaboration is *so* rare, but when I walked into a show, or a classroom, or a rehearsal, those odds rose dramatically. I was hooked.

About a year into studying improv, I had been practicing one night a week with a group for about a month. It was a mash-up of a few kids from my level 201 improv class at UCB, and some people I hadn't known beforehand. On this night, my friend Tim Martin (who we later had on *Broad City* as Dale, Ilana's creepy ex-roommate/lover) brought two new people into the group to practice, Ilana and her brother Eliot. They had taken a class with Tim, and he thought they'd fit in. Ilana and I were the only two women in the group, and I was convinced she was the actor that played Maeby on *Arrested Development*. I didn't know Alia Shawkat's name, and the show had ended by this time. I thought it would make sense that this girl had moved to New York and was getting into improv. I couldn't believe she was practicing with me! We all went to this bar afterward, Peter McManus Café, McManus for short. It was the bar everyone in the community hung out in, after every show, almost every night. On 19th Street and Seventh Avenue, it was, and I think still is, the improv community's Cheers. For years I was a mess in there, too nervous to talk to anyone not in my class at the time, too apprehensive to fully immerse myself in the scene. Like most adult scenarios, everything is high school all over again. So, it was the seniors, the cool kids, the ones on the house teams, the ones whose moves I studied at shows, sitting in the green booths in the back, sharing pitchers of beer, laughing. Slowly, over time, I pulled up a chair to those booths, got my own seat on the ripped, taped-over leather, and became a part of it all. But on this night, I wasn't there yet. I was still a noob, so my group and me sat up front as our teachers and coaches partied in the back. Ilana and I sat at the corner of the bar and hit it off right away. I told her I was from outside Philadelphia, and she told me she was from Long Island. Two of my best friends from college were from Long Island, from Smithtown. She could not believe it, she was from Smithtown! She bizarrely knew both of these people from high school and I quickly realized she was *not* Maeby. It feels false to look back on a moment, a conversation, and see an inciting incident of your own life's movie, like a formulaic Hollywood script, broken down beat by beat in a screenwriting handbook, but those handbooks sell so many copies for a reason! It was right there at the corner of the bar at McManus that my life changed completely. Ilana was so refreshing, this brassy girl with big opinions, bold, animated, and who seemed to know exactly who she was. And me, shy and insecure, pulling awkwardly at my clothes, outgoing only after a few drinks. There was a spark, a dynamic between us I had never experienced with another person, like she could see my potential self, sitting at the bar, and I, hers. She also *definitely* asked me if I was Jewish and didn't believe me at all when I told her I was. She made me laugh almost immediately. I'd been in New York for about a year, and I remember waiting for the subway on my way home that night, giddy—*this* was why I moved here, to meet people like her.

Ilana and I were friends for two years while we performed with this improv team. We called ourselves Secret Promise Circle. Sidenote: Improv team names for the most part, are *disgusting*. They are like TBTs of you in the first outfit you picked out for yourself: mismatched (but not in a cool way), head-to-toe tie-dye, etc. A choice you were proud of at the time, that turned into a humiliating and endearing blunder later in life. The seriousness of our team, of all the teams we were surrounded by, was both adorable and motivating. We *had to* take ourselves seriously. We worked day jobs we couldn't care less about—I had moved on to catering and assisting, the others had desk jobs, temped and waited tables in order to take part in this other nighttime gig. We paid coaches and rented rehearsal spaces and theaters by the hour and bought cheap liquor to give the audience (usually under fifteen people) free shots. We spent night after night in basements, testing the waters of our own courage in those underground labs, gaining the experience onstage to get better. And we *needed* to get better, all of us.

We performed a lot of shitty improv: embarrassing missteps, cocky showboating, wacky characters played nowhere near the top of our intelligence, and entire scenes performed in thick (borderline racist) accents. *Oy*. But every once in a while, there'd be a move or a scene or, rarely, an entire show that would kill. It would usually include one of us becoming someone else's life-size penis, but still! I rode the high off those moments for months. All of this, with the goal to become good enough to actually make money through comedy, to be able to quit the catering gig and do this for a living. That seemed unattainable, as I didn't really know anyone that had achieved it. I'd seen a few people from afar, the veteran improvisers who hung out in those back, green booths at McManus, slowly move up. I watched them in commercials and movies, saw them become performers on *SNL* or writers on sitcoms. Every time one of them broke out, it was thrilling. I *just* saw them perform at UCB, at the grungy basement theater in Chelsea, the theater I too was a part of. They were making it happen. If they could do it, maybe I could too.

Since I started at UCB, I knew, as did my peers, that the only path to success was to get on a Harold team. Harold teams are the theater's house teams. There were about nine or so Harold teams, each comprising eight people. I should also mention, for some *unexplainable* reason, there was almost never more than two women per team. Yes, there were more men at the theater and in classes, but this was a systemic problem, and a clear issue, like most institutionalized misogyny, that wasn't discussed or fought often or hard enough. Looking back, it's something I detest about my upbringing in comedy, the ingrained, uneven gender balance and lack of diversity that I did nothing to try and change. I didn't fit in yet, and was too enamored—and scared—of the community to call out its flaws. Now, in my work, I do everything I can to alter that balance.

These Harold teams were highly coveted to say the least, and those two slots silently delegated to women...seemed almost impossible to get. The teams performed a "Harold," which is the main format of improv you're taught as a student. A structure (about thirty to forty minutes) in which to play, that consists of three acts, or beats, where scenes and characters heighten to a place where ideally, they all weave together. The Harold felt akin to learning the foundations of representational drawing in art school: Once you can master that, the classic fundamentals, you can branch out. The Harold was developed in Chicago by Del Close and brought to New York by the UCB Four (the four founders of the theater). That last sentence is almost taken verbatim from the announcement made in the beginning of "Harold Night," every Tuesday at the theater, and is something I wasn't aware I'd memorized until just now. The audition process for Harold teams was brutal. It was done yearly, when new teams were created, and people on current teams were sometimes moved around or cut completely. The whole community became tense—the *perfect* vibe in which to be your funniest self! I auditioned three years in a row, and all three times I got a callback, but never made it onto a team. I knew in my gut I was good, that I was funny, but this was a yearly setback. I hadn't remembered how upset I was each time until my dad very recently and randomly said to me on a call after I told him about a new project in the works, "Bet they wish they put you on a Harold team now!" He held on to it longer than I had and I held on to it for...a while. Paul Downs and I still talk

one under mistletoe, trying to buy weed after a long hiatus, etc. The difference between our creative process then and now is simultaneously vast, and not much at all. We just finally managed to fit that egg observation into Season 4. We're not great at killing our darlings.

We came up with the name *Broad City* one night after work sitting on the floor of an aisle in a Midtown Barnes & Noble. I was now working at Birdbath bakery and Ilana at SkinCeuticals, and this Midtown location was midway for us and our commutes home, as most of our nighttime meetups tended to be. We had our notebooks ready and started throwing out names. I spewed out a string of potential ideas around words referring to women and words referring to New York, and Broad City was somewhere in the middle. Ilana stopped me. "Broad City," she said, "that's it."

The web series was the first time we were in complete control, and we attacked it full force. We wrote outlines and scripts for our two- to five-minute shorts and I drew the title cards and credits. We found local locations that would let us shoot on the cheap. We stole shots and used our own apartments. I had seen a post on the Improv Resource Center by our friend Rob who I knew from the community. He was looking to direct some projects, so we brought him in. He ended up directing and editing the first season of the web series and helped pick the theme songs we used, which were "Swing For Ninine," and "Django's Tiger," by Django Reinhardt, performed by the Cook Trio. The second season we found more collaborators, more people and friends in the community looking to direct and edit, shoot, hold a boom, or be in one of the episodes.

It was like a door opened, but one we first built and nailed into the wall. It was freedom. We paid people $100 or in pizza or bagels—apparently *Broad City* was born, and still runs best on, carbohydrates. We couldn't afford much, but as the show progressed, it gave these other collaborators experience, and content for their own reels.

The web series grew, as we experimented in style and voice, but we also grew our lives *around* it. By the time we were in the thick of making the *Broad City* web series, Ilana and I worked next to each other, making cold calls for Lifebooker, a group buying site and direct competitor to Groupon. This was the place that would eventually be the inspiration for Ilana's job on the show at Deals Deals Deals! We, however, actually *worked*, although making cold calls to salons and spas, encouraging them to discount their services by 50 percent, was one of my least favorite, and most anxiety-inducing, jobs I've ever had. Lucia Aniello, our main director and a writer on the TV version, worked there as well, across the room as a copywriter. Lucia worked there first then got Ilana a job, and Ilana recommended me. In between anxiety calls at work, Ilana and I planned episodes and punched up outlines over Gchat, and we'd shoot at night or on the weekends. There's a web episode that we shot at our desks one Saturday (I believe after convincing our bosses we needed access to the office to work), called, brilliantly, "Work." It was partially about how once you start wearing a padded bra, you can't stop or else everyone will know—we never veered away from those controversial issues. We released the show once a week on YouTube, breaking them up in two seasons over two years, and used all the social media platforms we could to share the web series with the world.

We took the show very seriously, even when it was only on the web. I got ahold of a PR friend's contact list and we reached out to bloggers to write about the show. We made a template that we used for outreach, saying how our content would be alluring to their viewers (for example, our web episode "Yoga" might appeal to any audience that was into fitness or parenting, etc.) and asking if they'd consider posting one or more of our episodes. It hardly worked, but the few times it did was worth me having two-thousand-plus contacts in my phone for the next eight years (I just recently went through and deleted them all). We threw finale parties at 92Y Tribeca, a space that sadly doesn't exist anymore, and started doing *Broad City Live* at UCB. I will never forget the morning a photo of us was in the *New York Times*, accompanying a piece about the Iron Mule Comedy Film Festival, where we were showing an episode. I bought a copy first thing in the morning and looked at it the whole subway ride to work. It was unbelievable, a photo of us, pointing at the mural on Houston and Bowery, was in the *New York Times*! I felt like everyone in the world could tell by looking at me; I was a woman with a web series, and my picture was in the paper!

The level of excitement contained within the little triumphs of our early years doing *Broad City* cannot be adequately conveyed. It's still there, between us, even now, almost ten years later. It's because we realized very quickly this show wasn't going to be just a stepping-stone. At first, we thought maybe this could get us hired as writers on something else, get us seen and possibly cast on another show, but once we harnessed our voice and realized how palpably fun it was to make this together, the show, even as a web series, was kinetic. It felt worth fighting for, to the death.

We had been working with a manager, Sam Saifer, for about a year. Getting representation in any form was a huge deal—and she really believed in us. She worked with Ilana first after seeing her do stand-up, and then Sam started working with me when she saw the web series. She lived in LA and was our first real connection to the industry. I had been working for years at shitty jobs and paying to take part in improv, so telling my parents I had a manager, even if that didn't completely make sense to them, was meaningful. Sam was young and hungry just like we were, and those early years with her felt so scrappy, in the best way possible. We were always hustling, always plotting and planning. Ilana and I were committed, and the web series was our main priority, but without having any real relation or experience to the industry, it would have taken us a bit longer to get there on our own. Sam thought it could and *should* be on television. There would be no *Broad City* without her.

It was the spring of 2011 and we'd planned to go out to LA that summer to take a leap and to pitch *Broad City* as a TV show. I had just quit Lifebooker after I sold three illustrations to AOL as part of their new AOL Artist branding campaign. (We ended up using this as a plotline on the show a few years later, except *Abbi* makes more money and accidentally draws something for a white supremacist dating site.) I had never sold my illustrations professionally, and the amount of money they gave me was a game changer at the time, enough to allow me to confidently put all my eggs in one basket. I often do that, put all my eggs in one basket—which is the main takeaway I got from my experience attending classes at Atlantic (actually from the required reading, *True and False*, which I did *before* I attended). It was something David Mamet wrote. To paraphrase: "If you have a plan B, you'll inevitably fall back on it." So, I avoid Plan B's. That lesson alone was worth the week of confusion at the school because it ingrained in me a belief in doing the thing I was setting out to do fully. I had a little bit of money, enough to quit my job and focus on selling the show. It felt very shaky, but thrilling.

We had made thirty-four web episodes, but we wanted to make one more. A finale. We had put more money into this one, and collaborated with our friend TJ, who was directing. He wanted to use higher-end equipment and raise the bar, visually, to feel more like a short film. We were invested and excited, and figured out a small budget and schedule, and then, almost immediately in the production planning, we experienced a streak of bad luck.

This episode, like most, was set to be shot outside, and bad weather forced us to push the date, which unfortunately made our main guest star unavailable. With a new shoot date, we needed a new guest star. I randomly saw a post online of Amy Poehler speaking at a gala in New York City that week. We had nothing to lose, so we asked her to be in the finale. Well, not technically. We didn't ask her *directly*. We didn't know Amy, so we asked one of our teachers, Will Hines, if he would consider reaching out to her for us. He was in and asked her if she would ever consider making an appearance in our web short.

And...she said yes! It was surreal to have Amy there—to meet her for the first time and begin to delicately explain how we were going to pour a crate of oranges on top of her, and then for her to get it and crack up. To make Amy Poehler laugh, well, there aren't many things better than that. Her laugh (a kind of cackle) is one of the best sounds in existence. We shot with her for an hour in the West Village on a perfect morning in May. The scene is of Ilana and I running frantically through the city on our way to get a cookie; we turn a corner and she runs into frame, joining us on our journey. In hindsight, that scene is exactly what happened, just replace the cookie for a career in comedy.

We went out to LA that summer to sell *Broad City* as a TV show, just as we had planned, but now we had Amy Poehler attached as an executive producer. After our web series finale came out online, we sent it to Amy, along with an email asking her, casually and gracefully, if she would like to be involved in producing our show. This email was drafted numerous times, the cursor held over the SEND button for dramatic effect. It was wild, we were asking *Amy Poehler* to produce our show?! (There were so many interrobangs at the end of thoughts, too many to list.) The worst she could do is say no, and we'd head out to LA as planned on our own. But then...she said yes, again! It was my dad's birthday, so I will always remember this day, May 21, 2011. I was at the beer garden in Astoria for a friend's birthday. It was the daytime and I guess the party wasn't poppin', because I checked my email. There it was, a response from Amy. She wanted to do it, wanted to make *Broad City* a TV show with us. Obviously, I immediately left the beer garden. I didn't say goodbye to one person. My first official Hollywood exit? Although a Hollywood exit is more like the opposite of an Irish exit, one where you announce your departure, making sure you, even upon leaving, are the center of attention. I raced outside on the street to call Ilana. I knew she couldn't have checked her email, or I would have gotten a call by now. She was upstate shooting an indie short and she rushed into the middle of a field to freak out. We screamed. I walked home on air. I *danced* home. Whether we would ever get to make a TV show or not, Amy had completely validated us, our voice, our potential.

We sold a script for a *Broad City* pilot to FX and developed that script for about a year. Then, after we got to a place we all felt good, it was handed up to the man in charge, the man we never met, the man at the top. He'd probably never heard of us, the show, or the year we'd been in development, and he wasn't into it. It was, as we were told, "too girly." So, they passed. We were devastated. This thing that was once so far-fetched had actually started to come to fruition, and then was abruptly taken away. I'm not a fan of "abruptly," as it's almost never a good thing—nothing wonderful happens *that* suddenly: "And then, the show was abruptly given a greenlight!" "His cancer ended abruptly!" "Then abruptly, they realized their love was meant to be!" Nope, it's always bad. I've had to develop a thicker skin for "abruptlys," but they still sneak in and catch me off guard.

Call me crazy, or naive, but this development process seems counterintuitive, outdated, and like a complete waste of time. Do I sound annoyed or heated by this snub, over six years later? Maybe, but maybe because I've been in the game a minute now and it keeps happening like that. Development for development's sake. Hard work kept at a certain level, aimed and focused in the direction of what the big boss's reaction *might* be. All to please one person. I suppose that's the vision of any given network, but that's a tough battle to win. Amy was our saving grace during this time—reminding us that we didn't want to make the show at a place that treated us like a bad boyfriend. She said we'd find a home for it, somewhere that really wanted it, and she was right. I am so thankful FX passed, because we then took our misunderstood, "girly" script over to Brooke Posch and Kent Alterman at Comedy Central and they got it and us completely. That year in development taught us so much about the business and about how easily things can end. The doors that have been shut, the ones I've walked away from, sad, frustrated, and depleted, have always somehow led to the other doors, the ones I didn't see right away, the ones that opened so many others. I have to remember this more often.

The six years between then and now have been completely transformational. We were so extremely green in the industry, so inexperienced and wide-eyed. We had never written for TV, never "broken" a story (where you crack the plot, the twists and turns in a script, etc.), never worked with a team of writers or within a strict time line of twenty-one minutes and fifteen seconds. Usually, to break the rules, one must learn the rules, but we didn't have any time to learn the rules. Our early episodes didn't follow a formula (they still usually don't); they were messy and raw, sharply focused on idea, and fueled by instinct. The show has always operated from Ilana's and my gut feelings. Not really knowing how the game works has allowed us to stay in it, to play it exactly how we want to. *Broad City* has been a complete education in every aspect of making television, of telling stories, creating a team and putting our heads together to dream up a whole world. The editing, the sound, the color, the communication between the network, our producers. Funneling our vision and other people's thoughts and feedback down to the last frame. It truly is a team sport, and we have the best team in town.

But it's my relationship with Ilana that I cherish most. We have such a strong partnership and have learned how we work most efficiently: I need coffee, she needs tea. When we're stressed, I pace around and use a weird neck massager I bought online that everyone makes fun of me for, and she knits. When we're writing together she types, because she's faster and better at grammar. We *actually* FaceTime when we're not in the same city and are constantly texting each other ideas for jokes or observations to potentially use (I recently texted her from Asheville: *girl with flip flops tucked into one strap of tank top*). Looking back now at over ten years of doing comedy and running a business with her I can see how our collaboration has expanded and contracted. But it's the problem-solving aspect of this industry, the producing, the strategy, the realizing that we could put our heads together and figure out the best solution, that has made our relationship and friendship what it is. Because that spills into everything. We both have individual careers now, but those other projects have only been motivating and inspiring to each other and the show. We bring back what we've learned on the other sets, in the other negotiations, in the other writers' rooms or press situations. I'm very lucky to have jumped into this with Ilana Rose Glazer, the ballsy, curly-haired, openhearted, nineteen-year-old girl that cracked me up that night at the corner of the bar at McManus. So many wonderful things have happened since we began working together, but there are a lot of confusing, life-altering things in there too, and it's such a relief to have someone who completely understands the good and the bad.

There's a look that Ilana and I have given each other over the last ten years in the middle of big moments, a silent but knowing, *How did we get here, how is this actually happening?!*: Catching our breath onstage at the first *Broad City Live* at UCB, in the middle of shooting that web episode with Amy and our initial breakfast meeting with her, in between details as we pitched the show to networks, moments later as we stole sodas and snacks from those network kitchens, the first day of every season's writers' room when we look across the table at our best friends right there with us, seeing Mike Perry's illustrated titles come to life for the branding of the show, when we knew we'd found the theme song ("Latino and Proud" by DJ Raff), when we saw the *Broad City* ads on the subway or painted on the side of a building on Lafayette Street, flying business class and sipping whatever orange juice drink they give you for free, when we saw Susie Essman next to Ilana on-screen, as we met Gloria Steinem or RuPaul, when Bill Cunningham took a photo of Ilana in a tuxedo as we filmed us riding down Fifth Avenue on Citi Bikes, when we shot on top of the Empire State Building in the rain, watching our real moms prepare to a shoot a scene in which they flip us off, as we danced on our float through the Pride parade, as Hillary Clinton walked onto our set, and during every handshake we give each other before we step or dance out onto any stage— that look is always there, a reminder of how far we've come, together.

I often wonder what the show and our lives would be like if we hadn't used our real names. In the pilot script we did for FX, my name was Carly, and Ilana's, Evelyn. I can't remember why we changed them from our own (it was Abbi and Ilana in the web series) when we originally sold the show, but I imagine it was to separate the characters from ourselves, to have a divide. We were in the office one day working on revisions, now teamed with Comedy Central, and one of our producers, Tony Hernandez, came in to tell us how strongly he felt we should use our real names, that so far, at least in the web series, using our real names was what made it feel so authentic. We agreed and changed them back. It would be Abbi and Ilana. A blessing and a curse for me personally. I'm quieter than my character, more shy—an introvert masquerading as an extrovert. It's the most flattering and affirming compliment in the world to have people believe my creation to be true, but a jarring realization to find, when I meet fans, that for as long as *Broad City* goes on, I'm living two lives, side by side. It's ironic that gaining some fame and success, that being known, makes the waves of insecurity and loneliness wilder and harder to navigate than ever before. It's uncharted territory for me, but it comes with the game. And I came to play.

We have known for some time now what the last scene, the last shot will be, but how we get there, I'm not exactly sure. What I am sure of is that this show, this fake world within our own, this project and this partnership has been and will always be a defining moment in my life. An extraordinary ten years. Ilana and I have had the privilege to allow ourselves to expand individually and together as creators, showrunners, writers, actors, producers, and directors within this project. We have matured as collaborators and learned to compromise and build a business together while maintaining our own autonomy. When it is over, I hope we walk away knowing we put all of ourselves into it—all our insecurities, our fears, all the messiness, the mistakes, the leaps and disastrous spills. I aspire for the show, and its ending, to be jam-packed with hope and heart and idiotic mishaps. For all fifty episodes to be overflowing with love and laughter from two knuckleheads who found each other's company constantly comforting through all of life's most unsure and empowering moments. I want to finish knowing we tried everything we wanted to, experimented in every way: through the comedy, the content, the characters, the medium, the style. I want to leave it all in the middle of the street, like a guttural howl at the moon. Our audience has watched us as real people grow up right alongside our characters. All four of us striving and failing, trying our best to find our places, our voices, our identity.

I don't know how I'll feel when it's all over. When we shoot the last scene, lock the last shot, or air the last episode. My chest gets tight even thinking about it—this has been the longest relationship I've ever had, and I know I'll be heartbroken when it's finished, but I also want it to end, I need it to. As much as I wish I could prepare and anticipate what that loss will feel like, I think I'll push it off as long as I can, to stay put, here, in the year I have left while living in Broad City.

The show has ignited a wild jolt of expression in me, and I will chase that energy the rest of my life. I can only hope I'll find something else that gives me what making *Broad City* has. Ultimately, that's the whole point of why I'm here in Santa Fe, on this road trip at all, searching for something to light my life up in a new way, like *Broad City* did my creativity. The problem with searching is you often find everything but the thing you're looking for. It's exactly like when you set out to go clothes shopping. If you announce that to anyone as your intention, even yourself, casually thinking, *You know what, I'm going to find a new top today*, you have immediately jinxed the task at hand, and you will find nothing. No tops for you! It will *never* happen. It's only when you are in the middle of something else, and you wander into a store, not looking for anything in particular, that you find the most fabulous fucking blouse the world has ever seen! Ideas, love, the rare spark of creativity, are all usually found, like that gorgeous blouse, when you forget about them for a moment and go about living your life. So, I kept walking. I ran my fingers along beautiful, handwoven textiles. I went to the Georgia O'Keeffe museum and wandered into her life for a few hours. I watched the light hit the earth-colored buildings, making them glow. I wasn't in some fake reality, on some back-lot in LA. It was real, and I was present, in a new city, on my own, and anything was possible. I had driven across the country and found myself in this particular place on earth. I was right *there*, in that moment in New Mexico, the sun shining down on my face. I didn't stumble upon a huge revelation that would lead to my next creative endeavor, or meet my next great love in Santa Fe, but before I knew it, I *was* buying a blouse, and sometimes that's exactly what you need.

Georgia O'Keeffe Museum

ADMIT ONE

THEY DON'T ACTUALLY GIVE
YOU A TICKET...

MY WOMAN

ANGEL

WORKING WOMAN

I work almost constantly.

I just took two conference calls, did an interview, listened to a cut of my podcast, gave notes, and had a phone therapy session (not work-work, but *work*). And I'm driving. I overcompensate to cover up the fact that I don't feel as fulfilled in other areas of my life. I tightly pack any spare time with projects and goals to be completed so as to not even have a moment to think about whatever deeper, darker, historical emotional patterns are buried under the surface. There's nothing in my life I can think of that gives me more satisfaction than checking off an item on my many work-related to-do lists, and I get a high from the starting and finishing of things. Creating something from nothing is the most engaged and connected I feel to myself and the world and yeah, in turn that has slowly made me more and more isolated. All of this will bubble to the surface in due time and I'll hopefully have an extra morning free before work to double up on therapy whenever it does, but I'm not trying to figure that out just yet. For someone who leans

on their career as a crutch, any holdups or hiccups in production become clear and build up over time, affecting said crutch,
and eventually have to be addressed. So, in an attempt to not
work for three weeks (but still, clearly work throughout), I've
started to conduct a self-review of some of my professional
insecurities... for the future, when I get back to *work*. I've made
a list (obviously).

Being the boss

I downplay the fact that I am the boss in my head, because, to be
honest, it sometimes scares me. But being scared of something
doesn't make it untrue. I am the actual boss. I embody that without fail on game-days, but in the locker room before we go out
onto the field (sports talk), I struggle with this. Ilana is more of
an outward boss, she sets boundaries and confidently makes her
expectations known. She loves it in the best way possible. I know
though, that she has an elaborate set of insecurities about this
too, as I have never met a woman, if they're being honest, who
doesn't. I don't think either of us needs a placard on our desks
stating that we are the bosses (instead, we demand trumpeted
announcements as we enter any room), but I'd love to get to a
point where I can just focus on the duties involved in actually *being* the boss, and stop worrying about the potential think pieces
questioning what it's like to be a "female" boss, about what people think of me *as* the boss. It's taken us a long time to be truly
taken seriously, to be left to our own devices, creatively. But our
gender is still almost always referred to before our job title.

Asking for things

I don't love asking for things. I do, however, ask for things almost constantly. I'm very good at asking for things via email. I bullet point items, tasks, etc. My alter ego on email is forthright, clear, and to the point. I'm great at detached demands, but when it comes to in-person requests, I feel like I'm in a yoga studio, just trying to breathe through it all without farting. Not actually farting, but you know what I mean. In a yoga studio it's so calm and peaceful and my main goal is usually just trying to not draw attention to myself in any way, like breathing too loud or making any sort of struggling noise. I suppose farting is always sort of in the back of my mind as a worst-case scenario. So, when I'm asking someone to give me more options, work on an assignment, grab me a coffee, or run an errand, in my mind, I'm spinning plates: Be respectful and kind, be clear with what you want, don't be a diva about the coffee, act casual, keep breathing, DO NOT FART, give them money—do they have money already? Is it rude of me to tell them to buy themselves a cup of coffee too? It's exhausting.

Telling people that something I asked for was not done correctly

There's a quiet epidemic of women taking and absorbing the blame for other people's mistakes, because of some inherent attribute deep inside us, constantly trying not to be difficult. I've had to learn to speak up and ask for what I want, specifically. And if it's not done right, I don't need to say, "Sorry, but..."

Why am I apologizing? Asking for what you want and need (nicely) is not being an asshole, it's part of the job. Whether it's a revision on a script, the look of a set, or the right coffee order. It's okay, and appropriate to insist things be done correctly.

Confidently saying no

Until recently, I've been afraid of saying no to things because for years, professional opportunities were few and far between, so I would say yes to almost anything. I'd take on every illustration project, or acting or voice-over job, even if I was working for free. I was so desperately seeking any chance to say yes, that saying no to a gig didn't ever cross my mind. But in the last year, I have been learning how to confidently say no. No for me now is all about making room for more Yes. So, while it feels insane to decline an audition or even a rare project being offered to me, because I remember when I was yearning for *anything*, I'm maneuvering my way through this more thoughtful approach to what I take on. I'm getting older and I'm learning more about myself and now I can say for certain that, no, I don't think a hair commercial on the beach in a bikini is right for me. No, I do not want to audition for that Woody Allen movie. No, I don't want to be the unfunny best friend that's one-fourth of an actual human being. I'll pass on that. I go back and forth on things a lot, but it's comforting to know I've nailed down most of my feelings toward bikinis.

Needing a second opinion

This one. I think this is the one women in the workplace are scared of. I know I am. *Broad City* is a very collaborative environment, and I trust everyone we've hired to work with us, so I naturally ask people's opinions. But when you get a new job, a new assignment, or a promotion, the fear of not being good enough, of not knowing everything can seep in. In the last season of *Broad City* (4), I directed two episodes. This was a new experience for me, and one I took very seriously. But I found, during the process, that a big insecurity for me is the fear that if I need a second opinion, that means I don't know what I'm doing. This is false, I do know what I'm doing, but it's that vulnerability, that want for another set of eyes on my decision that can make me shaky. I ultimately made all the decisions I needed to—after using my resources aka asking questions—but in order to do that, I had to continually let go of this unease that someone from a dark, back corner would pop out, pointing directly at me, yelling about how I'm a fraud for asking for help while in charge. That I'd be plucked up by a huge claw and dropped outside on the sidewalk, banished from taking on this new role. This fear is mindless. Understandable, but stupid. Crews are a team. Any business is a team, and the whole point of having people do different jobs and be experts in their specific department is for them to help in any way they know how. The director isn't there to bark out orders. They are the conductor bringing everyone's talents together to execute their own artistic vision. Asking and bouncing ideas off people, and even changing your mind, is allowed. It's so hard to ever show any sort of weakness, especially when you're a woman at the top of the project, in a business you never thought you'd actually be able to break into. But going through all the possibilities and asking for help is not weak, it's smart. I'm going to go ahead and dog-ear this paragraph so even I can come back and remind myself.

Celebrating and sharing my successes

I bought a house recently. I'm going to repeat that, I bought a house on my own, for myself, with money I worked very hard for. [Brief pause to jump up and down and pinch myself.] Even though I'm thrilled, I often find myself in situations where I feel guilt and shame surrounding this huge milestone in my life. I am really, truly proud of myself, but most of the time, I act like it's a secret. Single women buying houses on their own wasn't something I saw much of on TV or film growing up. That wasn't something unmarried women ever aspired to. It was always getting married and having babies, then the husband would buy the house. For the most part, it still is. In 2011, I went out for a drink with my friend Bethany. We were celebrating the fact that I had just gotten back from LA and had sold *Broad City*. I was about to tell Bethany the whole story over drinks, and our excitement was palpable. We took two empty seats at the bar, and Bethany says to the bartender, "We're celebrating!" Without a beat, the bartender looks at me and he says, "Congrats, you get engaged?!" I will never forget that. This was the biggest accomplishment thus far in my whole life, and I was kindly reminded that the default accomplishment for women is to get engaged. I love weddings, I love kids, and being a wife and mother are successes worth partying about. But come on, could you EVER imagine him saying that to two male friends that came into the bar to celebrate? It would have been assumed it was a professional accomplishment. I'm trying to navigate how much of this hesitancy to own these achievements is part of a social construct of gender, and how much is in my head. However often I feel shame about my successes, it's clearly not enough to stop me from writing about them...IN MY VERY OWN BOOK!

I'm done being polite about this bullshit. My list of professional insecurities entirely stems from being a young woman. Big plot twist there! As much as I like to execute equality instead of discussing the blaring inequality, the latter is still necessary. Everything, everywhere, is still necessary. The more women who take on leadership positions, the more representation of women in power will affect and shift the deep-rooted misogyny of our culture—perhaps erasing a lot of these inherent and inward concerns. But *whether* a woman is a boss or not isn't even what I'm talking about—I'm talking about when she *is*, because even when she manages to climb up to the top, there's much more to do, much more to change. When a woman is in charge, there are still unspoken ideas, presumptions, and judgments being thrown up into the invisible, terribly lit air in any office or workplace.

And I'm a *white* woman in a leadership position—I can only speak from my point of view. The challenges that women of color face in the workforce are even greater, the hurdles even higher, the pay gap even wider. The ingrained, unconscious bias is even stronger against them. It's overwhelming to think about the amount of restructuring and realigning we have to do, mentally and physically, to create equality, but it starts with acknowledging the difference, the problem, over and over.

Most men don't fear being difficult. They don't immediately and constantly have to prove themselves. Success is not something to hide or be modest about for them. I bet not one man has ever worried that having an assistant would ever classify him as being a douchebag, although I'm sure I'll get angry tweets (that I won't read—GOTCHA!) stating otherwise, but I'm speaking in "for the most parts." They are not worried what their successes will look like to the world, to their friends, to themselves. Men just do it, because they have been taught from before they could speak—sorry, before they were even an idea—that those things were theirs for the taking. That they are and should be in charge. But as people in charge, men don't have to be anything more than mediocre. I'm not saying all men are mediocre in any way, in fact I happen to know numerous (six-to-seven) extraordinary men, but in a competitive work environment, show me the number of mediocre men succeeding, versus the *zero* number of mediocre women at the top. Mediocrity isn't a part of the successful women's handbook, but I'm sorry, boys, for you it is. Women have to push harder, jump farther, stay later, think better, shit faster, all while trying their best to maintain whatever society says today their body should look like, how they should parent, what they should wear, when they should find love, what's inappropriate for them to do, say, be, feel, or fuck. The outward pressures are constant, but the inward congestion of doubts and insecurities are sometimes louder—women really can have it all!

THE COUPLES COUNSELING I
DIDN'T KNOW I NEEDED

ADULT CONCERNS

Duvet covers and how often to wash them
A sham? Throw pillows? Am I supposed to wash those things?
The entire political landscape
Climate change
Are we done for?
How to get equality
Racial equality
Gender equality
LGTBQIA equality
Candles? Are candles still in? I know for a while those smelly sticks were the new thing. I think also oils? Or wood sticks?

How to not only keep plants alive, but get them to thrive.

Is there a point in time where I'm supposed to do things like a neti pot? Do I have to?

Whether I'll ever be able to do a pull-up
Gun control
Heath care
Police brutality
Sexual harassment
Sexual assault
Representation
People without homes or food
How many terrible things there are to be concerned about
How to be a decent human being
How to waste less, and reuse more
What is really happening when we recycle?
Garbage Island being real and floating in the middle of the ocean
Where I should be donating money
Where I should be volunteering
Who I should be paying attention to
Clean water crisis
Oil drilling on sacred land and national parks
How to best use my platform
My feelings toward social media and my constant want to get off it completely
How to determine what needs to be dry cleaned, and what exactly dry cleaning is
How to recognize when I'm supposed to go to a cobbler to preemptively fix shoes before I've completely ruined them
Screens and how to stay off them while working primarily on them
Constant information and feeling the urge to be connected

How to get correct information
Making sure I take a break
Learning how to relax
Wars
Opioid epidemics
Refugee crisis
Famine
How much food we waste
Meditation
Figuring out how to learn how to meditate
Overall health
What's the pain on the inside of my right knee and how to make it go away
Eye doctor
Gyno
Dentist
General checkup
Dermatologist
Deductibles and if I ever hit them
In-network versus out-of-network
Are there other doctors I'm supposed to be going to?
All the different insurance you're supposed to have for all the things that could potentially go wrong in your body and every single thing you own
Which insurance to get when renting a car and when are you eventually going to make the wrong decision
Juice, and whether it's "over" or not
Feeling confident, body-wise
Which form of exercise is best for me, body and soul

Feeling confident, emotionally

Feeling confident, creativity-wise

Keeping in touch with family

Keeping in touch with friends

How to recognize relationships changing over time and be okay with it

How to manage multiple projects

Maintaining all hair removal upkeep

Remembering to stretch

Whether flossing once a day is enough

Are electric toothbrushes bad? Are normal toothbrushes back to being better?

Sneezing while driving and how to stay alive

Should I be smoking more weed?

Having the answer ready for who I'd invite to dinner if I could invite any famous people, dead or alive, to dinner

The way our country looks to the rest of the world

How disconcerting it is that so many people are hateful, anonymous trolls on the internet

If I can pull off hats

Finding a style

What brands I should be buying

What brands are terrible for the environment and humanity and should be avoided

That all brands might be terrible

How much sex everyone else is having

The fact that I don't know how to change a tire

That the electricity might just go off one day, like that TV show that got canceled almost immediately

If I should get back into running or not
How to figure out my hair
Wanting to learn another language
Contemplating taking up an instrument
Which salt is best
Diseases
Freak accidents
Memory loss
Not being present
Whether or not I will ever have children
Whether or not I will ever have multiple orgasms?
Whether or not I will ever eat a hamburger?
Nail (finger and toe) upkeep
Which eye creams and salves and gels are supposed to be applied to what, and when the applying is supposed to happen
When to throw out old creams and lotions
Bar soap or liquid soap
What detergent is the best detergent
How to properly wash bras
Buying bras
How to arrange bras in a drawer—do you fold them in half and invert one of the cups, or lay them out fully, one bra on top of each other.
Socks: folding, rolling or balling?
Wearing the right amount of makeup
How to apply makeup in a way so my face looks better than before I put it on
That I might walk funny and no one has the heart to tell me
I might drink too much seltzer and it will give me cavities

The time it would entail to get and use Invisalign

If I should be replacing my shoelaces every so often

The fact that every time I go to a concert, I end up wanting to leave before it's over

That I'm getting older too fast

That when my life is over, I will have not experienced all the things, not felt all the things

Death and dying and when and where and how

If scrunchies are back and why

RXBAR

3 Egg Whites
6 Almonds
4 Cashews
2 Dates
No B.S.
chocolate
sea salt

BEST FLAVOR
IN MY OPINION

PULLED OVER ON
THE SIDE OF THE ROAD
IN MONUMENT VALLEY
+ ATE THESE

GALA

NICK CAVE & THE BAD SEEDS
Skeleton Tree

DIY "AVO' TOASTS" OR "'CADO CAKES"
(RICE CAKES NOT PICTURED)

HOT SAUCE

CHOLULO

LEMON

SALT

ARTISAN SALT

Fleur de sel

AVOCADO

GRANDFATHER'S POCKET KNIFE

UTAH

It's come to my attention that I am not as spontaneous as I once thought. I am not a fly-by-the-seat-of-my-pants, wind-in-my-hair, roll-with-the-punches type of person. I don't often find myself saying, "Whoa, it's 3 a.m.—where did the night go!?," or "Give me your first plane ticket to anywhere." I like to know what's inside the Hot Pocket, I haven't let my gas tank drop anywhere near Empty in years, and not having a reservation at a packed restaurant but trying to get in anyway gives me heart palpitations. I'd never dare take a shot that is or ever was on fire, I look up addresses and scan driving route times the night before meetings, and I check expiration dates with my glasses on. With great comfort and ease come great amounts of preparation, limitations, and possible alternative routes brainstormed beforehand.

I wasn't always like this, I swear! I used to get blackout drunk, be okay with crowds, and often said and meant with enthusiasm, "You know what, surprise me!" I've slept in a ton of tents, my favorite Airhead flavor was the white one, and for a while there, I took mushrooms—for fun! What happened to me? Is this what your thirties are all about, entering deeper and deeper into the fear of unknown outcomes?

The older I get, the more anxious, more reserved, and more particular I seem to be becoming. I try my best to foresee anything that might make me uncomfortable, I plan, I micro-manage, I say no to things. But then, there's this other part of me, this sneaky side that keeps showing up. The Jekyll to my Hyde, or the Hyde to my Jekyll—I honestly don't know much about this reference other than it being two drastically different personalities and sides to the same guy (also a themed restaurant on Seventh Avenue that I've had mediocre drinks at). This rebellious outlaw is desperately trying to retain any sense of spontaneity, pushing me toward all the things that initially ter-rify me, like jumping off bridges (bungee jumping in Costa Rica), going for things that seem impossible (whole career), and putting myself out there (asking people out). That part of me, let's call her *Babbi* (which is what someone once *actually* thought my name was after I introduced myself), is why I'm on this trip in the first place. Without her, I probably would have stayed in Brooklyn and got some delicious chocolate chip cookie with salt on top every day, instead of driving across the country. This hypothetical cookie (clearly a real cookie, and one of the best I've ever had) would have satiated me temporarily but I would have stayed put, in all the ways. *Babbi* is fucking heroic! Thank whoever for Babbi! She keeps me on my toes and away from the cookies with the salt. But because of her, I also end up outside my comfort zone, in unwieldy territory—like falling in love or eating alone at a bed-and-breakfast. A wide variety of situations.

When I was planning this trip, one of the main things I wanted to find was space. Mostly space in my head, away from my usual day-to-day work life full of screens and emails, but also *actual* physical space. So far, my trip had been city-based, and usually involved me finding cute restaurants and wandering around, popping in and out of cafés and shops. Marfa had been more remote but was still a small town, and I'd known people there. I'd yet to really experience nature. I'd also yet to really challenge myself. I was on this trip alone, yes, but so far, I'd been staying in busy hotels or bed-and-breakfasts in mostly smaller urban areas, surrounded by other people. I had to force myself to go somewhere that kind of scared me at this point in the trip, and that kind of quiet and open space felt necessary. I'd been wanting to go to Utah for a while, hearing stories from friends who'd been to Moab, Monument Valley, and Zion National Parks, about the breathtaking hikes through the narrow stone canyons. I was hoping the distance from bright lights might allow me to release some of that unrest had been cluttering my mind.

Because my route so far was southern, I ended up picking Zion as it was the closest to my next destination in Arizona. On my way northwest from Santa Fe, I drove in complete silence through Monument Valley. I had to turn my music off, as nothing could pair properly with what I was looking at, the massive, ancient spires of stone, jutting up toward the sky. I wound my way up through the mountains, thirty minutes outside Kanab, to a lodge I'd found online. The website made it look incredible, and when I pulled into the parking lot, it looked exactly the same. I let out a sigh of relief, you never know how stuff you look at online is going to turn out in real life.

There was a main lodge, and next to it a small restaurant. Cows wandered inside a fenced-in area beside the main road that led up to small cabins, neatly nestled on a hill, overlooking the canyon below. I went inside the lodge to check in and noticed all the women were wearing traditional Mormon clothing—long-sleeved dresses in muted colors. *Right*, I was in Utah. Their clothing—along with their hair, braided or pulled back—was something I'd only seen on TV, but reminded me of the Amish women that worked in the local farmers market in my hometown, across from the stand my mom worked, selling homemade pastas. I felt bad that my immediate, gut reaction was negative, that these girls made me uneasy, but the wardrobe alone scared the shit out of me. You don't see a lot of images or representation of Mormons having fun in those long-sleeved, muted-colored dresses. It's always something horrible—some cult is being broken up, or women have been found in secret basements—emerging after years of being locked up. The woman behind the counter handed me my key—the keychain, a buffalo carved out of wood—and told me there was a TV in my cabin, but no cable. She showed me plastic drawers full of DVDs and said I could rent one for the night if I liked. I figured, when in Utah I should follow the local's recommendation, so, I borrowed a DVD of *My Best Friend's Wedding*. I had to, I was in Kanab!

I had stocked up on food the night before at the Whole Foods in Santa Fe. The guilt I feel toward the number of Whole Foods I visited along this road trip is real and alive.

There are so many local eateries and cultural mainstays I missed out on, but I opted for convenience and ease, like the privileged yuppie I sometimes check all the boxes for. I might as well have been on a mission comparing produce sections of the country's various Whole Foods locations— *Wow, they really don't like ripe avocados in Nashville...Austin is INSANE—too big to handle in one trip! Did you know it's the flagship?* ENOUGH ALREADY! I made dinner in the "kitchen area" of my cabin, which was really just the table closest to the sink. There was no cutlery provided, so I ran out to my car to grab my knife. Yes, I brought a knife...a pocketknife. My dad had given it to me—a small, decorative knife that my grandfather on my mom's side gave him a long time ago, my one piece of wilderness survival gear passed down through generations. He told me to put it in my glove compartment, for protection, but I mostly used it for romantically cutting apples while pulled over by the side of the road, overlooking a magnificent view (which I did on more than one occasion). I expanded the knife's repertoire to include cutting and slicing avocados for my famous (world-renowned) "'Cado Cakes," which is how Ilana and I refer to avocado toast on rice cakes. A delicacy that seems concocted specifically for a road trip, as no cooking is actually required, but I'd mastered this dish in my New York City apartment long before this journey.

I sat on the porch of my cabin and watched the sunset as I ate dinner, little pieces of dried rice falling everywhere, making a mess. The sunset was like a spectacle, a show you'd buy tickets to see—the rays of light burst out in a way I can't remember experiencing before. As I was taking it in, one of the women in the dresses crossed the large field in front of me, carrying cleaning supplies, and without even thinking, I ducked down on the porch. *What am I doing? She clearly works at the lodge! I'm being crazy.* I sat back up on the chair and pretended like I was cleaning up. What had Babbi gotten me into? I was nervous and scared, of what, I'm not exactly sure. I didn't think these women were going to harm me, not really, but the energy here felt *off.* You know when your hands get cold, but the rest of your body is fine, and you're not sick or *actually* cold, and you nervously drop to the floor at the mere sight of a woman in a long-sleeved, cotton, muted-colored dress and you worry maybe the avocado you just ate had gone bad or was harboring salmonella or *E. coli*, and it's starting to make you act funny, but then you're like, no way, that's so rare, and Whole Foods is a brand you trust even though it's a huge corporation and you shouldn't really trust them, 'cause they're taking over the world and controlling us in ways we have no idea about, but you can't seem to stop buying stuff from them—but all that aside, you just know deep down that things aren't right? That's how I felt. I didn't like being alone anymore. I wished I was with someone. I went inside, locked the dead bolt, drew the shades, and watched the shit out of *My Best Friend's Wedding*.

A few thoughts on the 1997 film *My Best Friend's Wedding*:

How was Julia Roberts's character such a respected and feared food critic by the age of twenty-seven? Is this possible?
They made a pact that if by the age of twenty-eight they

weren't in a relationship, then they would get married. *Twenty-eight?* What!? Twenty-eight was the low point where they would have to give up?

That scene where they're on a boat on the river that goes through Chicago, and they keep going under bridges, into shadow…and she has a moment where she could speak up— tell him she loves him, to marry *her* instead of Cameron Diaz— but she doesn't say anything…well, that scene just gets me every time. Come on! What's happened to Rom Coms like this?

What *are* the moves she's got that he's never seen?

Besides the fact that there's *zero* non-white people in the ENTIRE movie, and the one gay character is pretending to be straight and no one questions it, this is a classic!

Maybe it was my nerves about my surroundings or remembering Rupert Everett exists, but I couldn't sleep. After a few hours of skilled tussling, I figured reading a chapter in my book might lull me to sleep. But when I turned the bedside lamp on, the first thing I saw was that carved buffalo keychain on the nightstand. It's bizarre, the way our brains work, a visual cue can dart us back to the most random event. The memory the Buffalo took me back to is one I avoid, a night from my past I've pushed deep down into the dark hole of things to purposely not revisit. You'd think I'd be referring to the time my dad fell through the crawl space in my mom's garage when he was helping me move during college, when he landed on the floor and stared up at my mom and me, blankly (a stare I will never forget my whole life). When I sprinted inside the house, frantically looking for the cordless landline telephone to call 911, so he could be medevac'd to the hospital. [Sidenote: In an emergency situation, cordless phones are NOT COOL, all you want is a cord that leads you right to the phone.] But no, not going there tonight. You might imagine I'd be thinking back to when my parents got divorced, my teen years spent moving back and forth, my internalized emotion spilling to the surface—that must be the thing I was losing sleep over? No way, I might never figure that shit out! Instead, I'm referring to the time I couldn't throw a set of keys into a small panel of breakaway glass on an independent film shoot at four thirty in the morning.

Completely understandable and entirely relatable! Here we go:

I never refer to myself as an actor. If I meet someone and they ask me what I do, I usually say I'm a writer. This isn't false, I am a writer, but most people who know my work recognize me primarily as an actor. Don't get me wrong, I love acting. I want to be an actor and I'm on the prowl for opportunities to grow as one, but proclaiming it is almost always a hesitation. I am an actor. Why is that so scary for me? I think it's because whenever I think of actors, I think of Meryl Streep or Viola Davis or Tom Hanks, and then I'm like—I have the GALL to think I'm in *their* category? Besides my obvious insecurities, being an actor is terrifying. It means constantly putting yourself in other people's hands, inside other people's visions. When I was starting out, I would have done anything to get a part in a play, or a house team at the theater, or a shitty commercial. I remember audition- ing for a foot fungus commercial and being *bummed* I didn't get it! I was desperate to be a part of someone else's vision. I became a writer because being a working actor wasn't really happening—I had no control over my career being just an actor, and as I've said before, I enjoy being in control. So, in a bizarre turn of events, I ended up in the driver's seat of my acting experience by creating a part for myself, which is ex- tremely rare. But once you have that control, it's hard to let go of it.

Case in point, one of my first big projects as an actor for hire was an independent film called *6 Balloons*. It is mostly dramatic and deals primarily with heroin. I know, sounds right up my alley! But it was, in fact, right up my alley. The script for the film was written beautifully and the story was important. The opioid epidemic in our country is rampant, and I have known more than one wonderful human being who has died from a drug overdose. That experience, of losing friends so young, has stayed with me. This script, about an upper-middle-class heroin addict and his enabling sister trying desperately to save him, felt like something I wanted to be a part of telling.

The memory in question—the one that is keeping me awake in a cabin, thirty minutes outside Kanab, Utah—was during a week of night shoots for this particular film . . . in the middle of a production consisting almost *entirely* of night shoots. The film takes place over the course of one evening, so for nineteen days, we shot primarily overnight. Filming overnights for this long can make you feel like you're living in an alternate reality. You start work at 5 p.m. and get home at 5 or 6 a.m. The farther along into production, the more normalized this becomes: eating, "dinner" at 1 a.m., and waking up at 1 p.m. every day. It's bizarre. I'm not a fan, but it is one of the things I like about this industry—it makes you realize how many different kinds of lives you can live, not just through the stories told, but in the manner in which you can use the hours in a day. You can shift your life in many ways.

So, on this night, we were shooting a scene in which my character, Katie, borrows the keys to a pharmacy bathroom to help her brother, Seth, who is going through heroin withdrawal. It is clear that she needs the bathroom keys so Seth can shoot up in there with the needle she just bought. The pharmacist isn't happy, and they get into an argument, but she gives Katie the keys anyway, making a flippant remark about how she hopes Katie can remember to return them. Cut to later, they're back in the car and Seth hands her the bathroom keys they borrowed. *Shit.* After that whole thing with the pharmacist, Katie's gotta return those keys. She runs back to the pharmacy, but it's closed, and the doors are locked. She spots the pharmacist, but she won't even open the door so Katie can return the keys. What an asshole, right? So, Katie walks back to the car, then stops. Fuck this bullshit, and she throws the keys back at the pharmacy, smashing the glass front door. AHHHHHH— She runs back to the car and they peel out of the parking lot. Annnnnnnnd scene. What a thrilling, intense, funny, and exciting part of the film!

Sorry, spoiler alert. Now let's get into the throwing of the keys:

Earlier that night, the crew had put a rectangle made out of gaffer tape up on a brick wall near the set—the same size as the glass I needed to hit—so I could practice my aim. It wasn't an entire door I was trying to hit, but rather a top panel of break-away glass (approximately eighteen by twenty-four inches) that had been put in the door to smash. Breakaway glass, for those that aren't usually around fake smashes and crashes, is an in-dustry prop, used to create a more reliable outcome and a safer environment on set. I practiced and was doing well—I could hit the shape taped on the wall and I think everyone felt good about the scene we'd get to later that night.

Because it was a scene where we were going to break some-thing, even breakaway glass, it was shot last, around four in the morning. I was exhausted, but the scene was just physical, and I tend to be more nervous when it comes to dialogue-heavy scenes the later it gets, so I felt okay. I had prepared before-hand, *like I do*, and could hit the mark—what could go wrong? Then we began what would be an hour or more where my body completely betrayed me. I COULD NOT FOR THE LIFE OF ME HIT THE GLASS. I threw the keys to the right of the door, to the left, hit the sidewalk in front of me, the lamp above the PHARMACY sign. I chucked them at the curb, the window, the metal rim around the roof. It was absolute insan-ity. Forty crew members watched me throw those keys every which way *except* where I was supposed to. They watched me fall apart. My confidence was gone entirely. It was like my body was the only one honest with me—it screamed, "You're a terri-ble actor and we're not gonna help you! We're ruining this for you, for your own good. We're cutting the power, you're on your own you talentless, idiotic dumbass! You think you're an actor!? Meryl would be able to hit that door with her eyes closed. Go home you stupid comedy writer!"

At least ten different people in the crew came over to tell me how I should throw the keys—mostly men. THANK YOU! I know how to throw stuff—I used to play softball and I think I'm pretty athletic—but this was absolute mayhem. No one could help me. I completely lost control of my body. My mind was no longer connected to my arm or my eyes. With each throw, the clunky metal object on the keychain started to break, pieces of it falling off. I must have thrown the keys at least thirty-five times. We were running out of time—the sun was coming up! I could have died. I don't know how I didn't. It went on forever. A part of me thinks maybe I *did* die in that moment, on that night, in the middle of one of those throws, maybe I died and it's all been a dream since then? In the end, I threw the keys and hit the glass, but I was standing SO embarrassingly close to the door, it's unbelievable I came back to work the next day.

That overtaking of my body and my inability to use it for what I needed carried such a weight. Because this was physical, happening so publicly, and at the same time so internally, I can feel it again, can bring back that humiliation, that complete lack of control. But it was just throwing keys at a door. No one died, no one was even mad, we got the shot! It wasn't a big deal to anyone but me. So why do I even care, almost two years later? Why does it make me cringe to even think about, and how can a buffalo carved out of wood on a keychain on my nightstand bring up those feelings so randomly? Memories fascinate me, how they gain or lose weight over time, always fluctuating, just like our bodies, becoming lighter or heavier the more they need attention. That night and my inability to throw those stupid fucking keys reminded me just how shaken I've been the past six months, how no matter how hard I tried, I couldn't get over this heartbreak, couldn't stop feeling insignificant in general or shitty about ways in which I could have reacted differently. I could probably throw those keys and hit my mark right now if I had to (I will *not* test this theory), but I was again in a place where I was unable to do what I knew I needed, to move on. Physically I was fine, but my mind and heart, emotionally, were not, and no new environment or vast amount of space in the sky was going to fix me. It was just going to take time. I thought driving as far away from my life as I could would release the things I was struggling with, but it seems I'd come all this way only to drive more directly into them.

As I lay awake in bed, staring at the ceiling, I suddenly felt the urge to go outside, to overcome my fear of actually being alone in the middle of nowhere. I debated if I should go and see what it looked like out there at night. On one hand, I knew the sky would be incredible and I might regret not experiencing it, but on the other hand, were there wild animals outside? There are huge birds out west like condors—do they prey at night? Also it was easier and way more comfortable to stay safely in my bed, I'd probably only tussle for another hour before I fell asleep—and just like one of the most thrilling, final scenes of a romantic comedy made in the late 1990s, Rupert Everett's silky British accent provided an answer:

And then, she was up, out of bed in one exquisite movement, wondering, searching, sniffing the wind like a deviled deer. Has God heard her little prayer? Will Cinderella dance again?

I put my shoes on, walked outside, onto the porch and down the stairs to the grass. I kept going, farther and farther into the field, tightly clutching the wooden buffalo keychain until I was far away from my tiny cabin I'd felt so isolated inside. There wasn't a woman in a long dress out in that field ready to get me, that's not what I was afraid of now, it was the silence and the darkness that scared me. I slowed down and stood in place. The only thing I could hear was my breathing, in and out, in and out. There were no lights, no sirens, no generators humming, no trash trucks and no subway rumbles through the walls, no groups of drunk friends stumbling outside my window, no light from the TV, no helicopters circling. Nothing. No one. Finally, for a moment, I was just, right there. I stopped looking back at what I could have done differently in this relationship, stopped replaying scenes and rewriting new endings that will never happen. I wasn't stressing about all the things I needed to do for work, all the calls and the emails, all the lists I make to try and occupy my mind. I wasn't worrying about *Broad City* ending, how we'd do it right, or how I'd feel once it was over. None of that. I just stood there looking up at the sky, not remembering, not worrying, not planning.

The stars out there, out west, are different, they're brighter and bolder, and they make you feel that the world is so much more than you ever could have thought, that maybe you'd only been focusing on a tiny little corner. I know all those stars are there too, in my New York sky, but I don't see them. There's too much in the way. This was the space I was longing for and had been seeking out. But I could see now I hadn't been yearning for that expanse to escape into, but rather to remember that I was a part of it. *Right*, the universe. *Right*, the sky, the stars, the unfathomable mystery of those faraway galaxies. The original, intended purpose for the word *awesome*. How had I forgotten about all this? It's all right here.

I tried to imagine what I might look like from a star's perspective: a tiny person in a grassy field in southern Utah, all by herself. She just stood there in her mismatched pajamas, looking up, so much happening in the world around her. But there she was, awake in the middle of the night, quietly staring away from it all, letting time slow down for a moment.

THEY WERE 28 YEARS OLD!

WHERE'S HE BEEN?

THIGH GAP

NOT ONE PERSON OF COLOR IN THIS FILM?

KEY TO MY CABIN, OUTSIDE KANAB, UTAH

DRIVE DOWN TO SEDONA

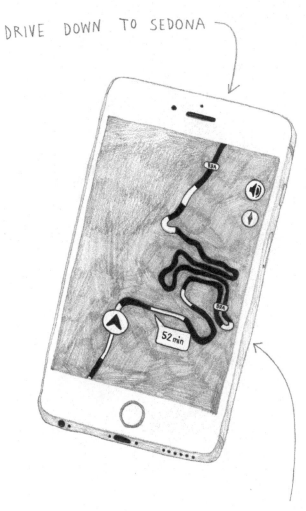

...OOOK

SEDONA SPIRIT

I've never been intensely spiritual, but I definitely dabbled.

There's a church in Brooklyn Heights that I refer to as "my church," which is bizarre as I don't attend this church and I'm fully Jewish, but this building is, or was, when I lived nearby, a tiny scratch in my spiritual itch. On the outside, there's a message board behind glass—one that on other churches would usually list the service schedule, but mine puts up quotes, and changes them frequently. I would go out of my way to see what quote might be posted, sometimes riding a less convenient subway line so I had an excuse to walk by it. I needed that little boost, that lift in my spirit. The quote might be from James Baldwin or a pope, other times it was Sheryl Crow or Janet Mock. Whoever it was, whatever they said, I forced myself to stop and think about it. I miss those brief, holy moments in front of my church on Henry Street. There's a church in my neighborhood now that has a similar board out front, it lists information about their services and has a quote from the Bible: *Love is Patient, Love is Kind.* After the third time I passed by and realized it was permanent, I became angry. *IS IT THOUGH?* I have avoided this church ever since.

In the last six months leading up to this trip, I had been leaning into these attempts at mindfulness and spirituality. Between the breakup, my newfound sexual awakening, and *Broad City*'s end being in sight, I could feel my life changing significantly, in larger, more sweeping ways than I'd ever experienced, and I was scared I was spinning out of control. There was a looming sense of the unknown, and because of that, my spiritual dabbling doubled.

I read horoscopes from time to time for fun, listen to anything Oprah puts out into the world, and at one point in my life *The Alchemist* was my most treasured book, so I wasn't unfamiliar with seeking some guidance, but this began to feel more intentional. I started doing yoga and eating mostly vegetarian— trying my best to focus on foods that have lots of nutritional value instead of lots of bacon. I'd also been given more stones and crystals from friends than I know what to do with. Each was supposed to attract more of one thing and ward off another. I have them placed around my house, on windowsills and on shelves, in pockets of book bags and on my nightstand—more a reminder of my kind friends' powers than the crystals'.

Despite my best efforts, I was still hanging out in the spiritual novice section, and I needed to cut the bullshit and get down to business. So, when planning this road trip, I decided to go to Sedona. If I was going to go mystical, and fully give that "woo-woo," "hippy-dippy," "cosmic moon cycle" arena a fair chance, Sedona was the place I was going to do it.

An hour into day 1 at the luxurious, campus-like beast of a resort tucked inside a red-rock canyon, I surrendered to the amenities and found myself a plush-slipper-wearing, kale-chip-eating, energy-vortex-searching soul seeker. I'd completely given in to the Teslas (there were a bizarrely high number of Teslas). I tore open the schedule of activities I found on the desk in my room and cracked my wrist—the equivalent to knuckles for me. Watch out spirituality and calming essential oils, I'm coming for ya! I was going to leave this place strong and stable, just like the red rocks—my mind clear and peaceful, my heart open and no longer aching. What an incredible three days this was going to be—PEACE AND QUIET AND SPIRITUALITY AND LOVE AND LIGHT AND LOVE AND LIGHT AGAIN AND RED ROCKS AND JOY! Also, this place was ridiculously expensive—I was going to get my money's worth.

I called the concierge to book activities, but they encouraged me to come to the office and go over everything. In-person interaction, especially when it's about bettering myself, is *just lovely*—it's one of my favorite things to do and I didn't hesitate one bit! (Please sense my sarcasm.) I walked over to the lobby (a quarter mile away) and sat down with a concierge to organize the next three days of the rest of my life. She was dressed head-to-toe in wilderness gear, wearing one of those safari hats that tied up from both sides. The overcompensation of gear is usually a deterrent for me, a clear case of something being bullshit as I'm not usually in a place where an extreme amount of gear is necessary. But I was trying. I would let this go and continue on my road to enlightenment! Spirituality comes in all shapes and amounts of wilderness gear, who was I to judge? I began to list off my plan, and she tried to keep up. I felt like I was one of those rich ladies who goes into a store and buys things in more than one size all at once, to try on at home, just because she can, except instead of high-rise denim, I was trying on every which way of raising one's endorphins and emotional well-being.

When Conci (nickname for concierge—*CATCH UP!*) handed me a printout of my program, it looked like an eager honor student's after-school schedule, jam-packed and overwhelming for no apparent reason. Yoga classes, aerobics, abs workouts, a massage, hike after hike. My time for the next three days would be carefully and densely filled with healing exercise and body-enriching activities. Who cares if my relaxation felt like a micromanaged TED conference for one?! Nothing says tranquility and enlightenment like a hard-core itinerary.

The next three days I stuck to my schedule: went to exercise classes back-to-back, explored the various trails on the grounds, and read by the pool (not on the original schedule, but added later in pencil once I found out about the pool). By night I'd go get food from one of the many restaurants inside the large main lobby. I had been told by almost everyone that worked there (mostly the hosts I stared at while I waited for my to-go order) that I *must* try the prickly pear margarita, so I did. *Eh.* I took a mountain bike tour through the red rocks one morning on one of those supped-up bikes with the shocks that you see in magazines but don't think you'll ever ride in real life. Two married couples and I slowly wove our way down paths, through rocks and crevices, as our mountain bike guide George spewed instructions that doubled for life advice. Yes, we *do* have to look through the obstacles in order to get past them! If we look down and focus on the rocks and other things in the way, we *will* fall! We have to point ourselves in the direction we want to go...on the trail. Yes, George! I was fully on board with this intense metaphor of a mountain bike ride and hung on to his words as tightly as my handlebars.

I went on a solo hike through the valley of red rocks, sat in a meditation room, briefly (I didn't know what to do in there...), and climbed a path to a stone energy vortex. Vortexes are sacred areas that are thought to hold very powerful, healing energy, and leave you feeling different than when you came. Sedona is said to be a vortex itself but has within it even more powerful centers of energy. I stood at the vortex, shut my eyes, and waited. *Here we go!* It began to drizzle as I stood there—okay...could this be some sort of energy symbol!? It hadn't rained in days, and then the moment I get to the top of the trail and touch the stone vortex it starts to rain? Timing *is* everything. As I continued trying to force the rain to mean something, it started to *really* come down and I had to leave in a rush, retracing my steps through the maze of trails to the hotel, hoping I remembered the right way back. I *did* leave the vortex in a different state than when I came, so that was true.

Besides the energy vortexes, which I clearly conquered, I had heard getting one's aura read in Sedona was essential. I couldn't leave without a photo of my aura! The hotel itself was the kind of place you never needed to leave—but I wanted to drive into town and see what *actual* Sedona looked and felt like, plus, that was where all the aura reading places were located.

At first glance, the town appeared to be a larger version of the boardwalks I remembered visiting at the Jersey Shore, the kind of place where everyone might be buying T-shirts that said I GOT STONED IN SEDONA. The only difference was the red rocks peeking over all the rooftops, immense nature rising into the periphery. Getting one's aura read seemed so personal, but this place seemed so public, a true tourist trap.

Although I hadn't gotten an aura photo, I had been to a couple of psychics before. In high school, my friend Sam's mom hired a psychic to come and read our palms at her sleepover. I remember feeling like I had given her too much information. I got excited in response to anything she said: "The letter *M*...hmmm. My grandmother's name starts with an *M*!? Wow, that must be it." I'd make any connection from my own life to whatever she said. I wanted an experience, for her to find something I didn't know about myself. To tell me what was going to happen. The other time I went to a psychic was one of those days where you have the strong desire to punch someone right in the gut. Years ago, my manager (at the time) was able to secure me an appointment with her beloved psychic, which was difficult as this woman was one of those renowned LA psychics, someone the Kardashians or Real Housewives might go see, so apparently in high demand. I was nervous, not knowing what to say or do with a clairvoyant, let alone a famous one. My experience in high school wasn't successful and I wanted to do it right this time. Do you talk first or let them do the talking? Am I supposed to have questions ready? On top of that, I was running late.

I *hate* being late. I treat myself like that friend who is always

late, so you tell them a meeting or dinner starts a half hour before it does, hoping they end up actually on time, except I'm
both people in the story. I coyly remind myself to show up
thirty minutes early. I plan up the wazoo. But not on this day.
Los Angeles is known to be tricky, driving-wise, but what they
don't tell you, what they leave out of the story, is the parking. One of the true untold stories of Hollywood. *Lifestyles
of the Rich and Famous: Parking Predicaments, Uncensored!* The
extra time, even if you're going to a parking lot, can be significant, and must be factored into your planning. When I'm in
LA now—maybe due to this incident—I always look up the
parking situation, and it has saved my ass on numerous oc-
casions. My manager's fancy psychic was located in Beverly
Hills, obviously, and when I could see I was going to be at least
fifteen minutes late, I called my manager and she said she'd
call the woman to let her know that traffic was out of control
and I'm from out of town. The parking structure next to the
psychic's building was backed up and I was slowly circling up
floor by floor, looking for an available spot. Finally, I'm running
down the hallway to her office door, passing doctor's office after doctor's office (weird she's next to all these doctors?), where
I calmly composed myself before knocking. The door opened,
and I began to apologize profusely.

The famous Beverly Hills psychic was probably in her late
fifties or sixties with a thick accent I couldn't quite place.
She looked like she would maybe work in a high-end department store, one of those women that is mean but works on
commission—a confusing duality. She took one look at me and
wouldn't do it. Even though we had forty-five minutes left, she

would not go through with the session. She coldly stared at me and proceeded to give me no explanation, other than that I was fifteen minutes late. She made me leave immediately, slamming the door in my face. I was so pissed. What a fucking dick. I remember then nervously thinking maybe it wasn't about my lateness. Maybe she saw something in me she couldn't bear to reveal, something about my energy she didn't even want to touch—like I might die soon or be involved in a terrible tragedy. After that, I decided palm readings, tarot cards, and psychics in general maybe weren't for me. I had enough pre-drive planning and parking rage to deal with for the time being.

Sedona was going to be different than these previous mystical endeavors. I had set aside a few days to specifically stay in one of the most spiritual places in the world—I was going to open myself up to the powers that be. My road trip was almost finished, and I wanted to look at myself in a new way—to try thinking about my energy and what I was putting out there.

I found a crystal shop by googling "Sedona aura reading," so in a way I was offering myself to Google, the all-powerful, all-knowing. It had four and a half stars and good reviews, and because I wasn't even sure what to look for, the fact that people even left reviews made me feel good. I often doubt my ability to choose a good restaurant or bar or store online, but this trip was proving me wrong. In each city, I'd managed to find the exact type of coffee shop I was looking for, the perfect lunch spot, most ideal indie bookstore. I now harnessed the talents to find what I was looking for—at least store-wise. The shop was cute and filled with display areas of stones and crystals, oils and spiritual reading material. A bunch of other people browsed throughout the store as they waited for their time slots, which made me feel confident I'd made a good selection. I had clearly hit the jackpot again! I spoke to a woman behind the cash register, who set me up for an aura reading appointment and photograph, and then a tarot card reading and aura evaluation. I had no idea what this entailed, but I was there to go hard-core mystical or go home. Or rather get all the items on the menu that the woman at the counter suggested.

I wandered around the shop for fifteen minutes until my appointment time, anxiously thinking about what would possibly be revealed in this aura photo; *it was going to be great, a color around my head will give me some insight—maybe make me understand my current state, maybe something about the anger and frustration I'd been feeling constantly toward myself and my inability to bounce back to any form of normalcy. Sweet. Yeah, this was a good idea. This was gonna be fan.tas.tic. My aura might be a color that would acknowledge how hurt I'd felt or how I was scared to land in Los Angeles because then what? Then I'd really have to move on. Would that be like a red hue? This was good. Yeah. Great. I love spirituality and crystals—they're all over my house, just like this shop! I don't feel any pressure—All. Is. Good. I feel wonderfu—* and just then the woman I made the appointment with earlier, over at the cash register, found me—it was my time. Phew, that could have gone on for a while.

She looked like a librarian from my elementary school, crunchy with a friendly smile as she escorted me into what I can only assume was once a storage closet. This was right off the floor of the shop, and I could hear other customers chatting about potential purchases as she pulled the curtain (instead of a door) closed behind me. Once inside, my eyes adjusted to the fluorescent light to see a desk with a Dell computer on top. She had me sit at the desk and she leaned over my shoulder as she walked me through the instructions to the program on the computer. I could barely hear her over my screaming inner monologue: *HOLD UP, THE READING IS ON THE COMPUTER!?? A COMPUTER AURA PHOTO!? ALSO, YOU DO THE AURA READINGS AND THE CASH REGISTER? THIS IS A HOAX! WHAT DO YOU THINK, I'M A COMPLETE IDIOT!?* I wanted to leave, but what would I say? What if this woman owned the crystal shop? What if this was her family's company and it had been passed down through generations? What if they were barely making ends meet and that's why there wasn't a door in here anymore? Doors are the first thing to go! What, am I gonna stand up and call her out on this half-a-room, fake-spirituality-meter moneymaker when she just had to sell the door to pay rent? No, I couldn't do that to her. I would stay, and stick it out for her grandparents who built this place from the ground up, one crystal at a time.

She instructed me to put my hand on what looked like a computer mouse from 1999—you know when there seemed to be a race for which company could design the ugliest, most ergonomic mouse for your hand to rest on all day? Then she said I should look straight ahead and follow the prompts on the screen. She left me alone and began the program. I was surprised how angry I was, sitting in this closet. This was the thing I *had* to do in Sedona? What complete bullshit. I knew it. I thought there'd at least be some old-timey, under-a-cape-type camera, a relic from the past that could see into my soul. Instead, I looked into a ten-year-old computer camera, Velcro'd to the screen of an old Dell desktop. I thought I'd get an actual photograph, not a terrible, faded color printout from Staples' most popular Brother printer. I could have done this at home, online! I could have just googled "at-home aura reading"! I was disappointed. It felt like an obvious scam. If it had been an actual photograph, developed in a darkroom by a woman who looked like she'd been alive forever, would that make it more real? Honestly, *maybe*. Optics are important, especially in the world of believing in something you're trying to not be skeptical about.

I had a few minutes in between the aura photograph and the rest of my reading, so I went to use the ladies' room. One thing you shouldn't do in the middle of any sort of mystical experience is use the restroom. The bathroom was also the *actual* storage supply closet, clearly the new home for the supplies that probably once lived in the "Aura-Reading Room." I don't know what kind of bathroom would have felt more appropriate, but seeing the psychic's lunches and random mugs in the tiny kitchen on the way back from the bathroom made this all too grounded in reality. Who were these women who lived such normal lives back here in this little kitchen, only to read other people's auras all day?

I cannot remember the name of the woman who brought me upstairs for the next portion of the reading, but I'm going to call her Deborah. *Deborah* feels too generic and I'm worried it might be her actual name, so I will now be referring to her as Flo. By the time Flo and I met downstairs in front of a basket of tiny blue stones selling for $10 a pop, I was done. I was not eager to solve my problem here anymore. I was over this place as the path to some sort of insight about whatever I'd desperately been looking for. I wasn't going to find myself by analyzing a purple hue surrounding my head in a photo. This wasn't real; the vortexes in the rain, the mountain bike metaphors, all my friends' crystals sucking whatever bad vibes out of my bedroom at night, the very brief time spent in the meditation room—it was all nothing. The psychic in Beverly Hills didn't see some negative energy in me she couldn't bear to reveal, she probably just wanted to take my money and eat her lunch. I wanted to get out of there and go eat kale chips by the pool and forget I even tried this hard, but my fear of confrontation wins in scenarios like this, so I kept my appointment with Flo, not wanting to try and navigate explaining why I didn't want to continue. She escorted me upstairs into a little room where she asked me to sit at a small table against the wall. She sat across from me and paused.

"I'm going to invite Jesus into the room to help guide us," she said.

Ooookay. I nodded with approval. Sure, do what you gotta do. I knew going in I wasn't going to give her anything, not one bit of information about myself. I wasn't gonna get duped by showing excitement over a letter in someone's name or her sensing a "new beginning" in my life. You could say that to anyone! Not today, Flo! She looked through my file of printouts from the aura reading downstairs, my "extensive paperwork," and nodded, "Hmm." Ugh, this was so ridiculous—my paper-work was in a bright-blue folder, and she all of a sudden felt like my language arts teacher in fourth grade. She turned to a chart highlighting the chakras—or energy centers in the body—and proceeded to tell me my heart chakras were low, and my throat chakras (the ones that are used to communicate) were very, very low. I *did* feel that way. I sat there listening, stiff as I could be as a tear fell down my cheek. *Abbi… Stop.* Then more tears. How was I crying in this room right now? *Stop it!* This photo and these measurements were taken on some app on a shitty Dell computer in half a closet! And to make matters worse, I was crying not only in front of this stranger but apparently, Jesus Christ himself! But I couldn't help it. She was exposing what I'd been holding so tightly for so long. This part of myself I'd been trying to hide, the thing I avoided communicating to any-one: that I might be right back where I started, unlovable and unable to love. I felt truly alone and might remain that way.

Flo passed me a box of tissues and asked me if I had any specific questions, and I didn't. I couldn't think of anything, I couldn't even speak. I sat there quietly, frantically fighting to preserve any dignity I had left, as if speaking might unleash a new level of tears I wouldn't be able to rein in. I took a deep breath as she began the tarot reading, placing one card on the table at a time, and with each explanation, Flo was breaking me down against my entire will. I was falling apart, and I couldn't stop. It was as clear as I was afraid it might be, I wasn't hid-ing anything. This woman stared me in the face and told me I needed balance. She made direct eye contact as she said I had made my entire life about work, and that it seems I had given

CRYSTALS I BOUGHT IN SHOP IN
SEDONA AFTER SURPRISINGLY INTENSE
AURA READING:

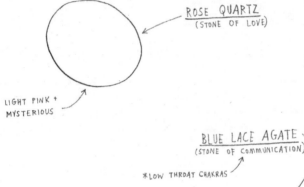

ROSE QUARTZ
(STONE OF LOVE)

LIGHT PINK +
MYSTERIOUS

BLUE LACE AGATE
(STONE OF COMMUNICATION)

*LOW THROAT CHAKRAS

LIGHT BLUE

NOTE 1: THESE WERE RECOMMENDED TO ME

NOTE 2: I CAN'T DRAW CRYSTALS

PRICKLY PEAR MARGARITA

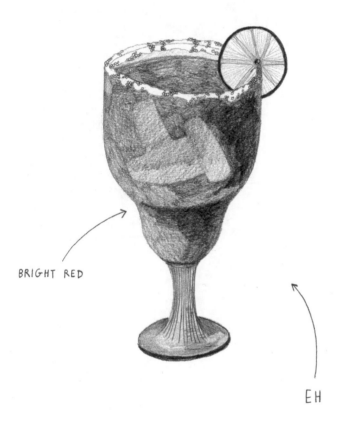

BRIGHT RED

EH

SEDONA SLEEP STUDY

Alarm set on phone: 8:00 a.m.
Do Not Disturb: on
Brainwaves App: Set to—DEEP SLEEP / Rain and Thunder—
for 30 minutes
Lights: off

11:09 p.m.

Shit, there's light seeping in from the curtains.
And the red light from the TV.
And the alarm clock. Just let it go, it's fine.

No, it's not.
I have to eliminate the light!

How does anyone sleep with all these distractions?! I guess people wear those face masks that block out all the light...I just
don't like the elastic bands on my head all night—I never know
if they're supposed to go over or under my ears and I'm always
so disoriented when I wake up after wearing them.

Yeah, not for me.

Maybe hotels put out so many different-size towels so you have lots of options to cover up light sources in the middle of the night. Washcloths are perfect for the red light on the TV, the medium-size towels that aren't clear exactly what they're for (too small for putting hair up in, too big for a washcloth) are perfect to cover the alarm clock, and a large towel is great for the sliver under the door leading into the lit-up hallway.

Perfect.
Taken care of.
Taking care of business, all night. *Taking care of business co-vering the lights!*
Hahaha.
Ohh my goodness, I am so annoying.

11:22 p.m.

Good, darkness.

Hand towels! They're hand towels.

11:30 p.m.

I should be writing more on this trip, I'm missing out on the opportunity to get everything down on paper. I can't seem to find my process. What do other people do? Other writers and artists seem so sure of themselves. They probably don't lie awake in the middle of the night in hotel rooms by themselves singing pop songs from the '70s, making the words their own. No, they probably fall asleep immediately and dream all night, and then wake up, inspired by their fantastical dreams that have clear metaphors that prompt them to get lots of inventive writing done. They probably wake up and immediately go to work—so many dreams to rehash—sure, they need coffee too and go on walks too and have ebbs and flows of productivity just like me, but I bet they are on more rolls. I wonder how I can get on a roll? What do those effortlessly productive writers' work spaces look like? Some are probably really cluttered with books and scraps of paper full of inspirations that had to be written down in a frenzy. Their walls are probably covered in friends' artwork, things to motivate them. I can't live like that—the scraps of paper everywhere, I'd spend all day cleaning it up, too distracted by all the notes I'd jotted down. Maybe some people have a sort of blank space so they can only focus on the task at hand. Minimalist. That's sort of what my space is like now, except it's like that because I can't seem to commit to art on the walls and haven't put things up. I need to be able to commit, even if it's just to artwork on the wall! I've always wanted a standing table, where I can make lots of hands-on projects. I don't really work with my hands much anymore. I will, soon, get a higher table to stand and work at. That's a good idea.

I have to remember that, high table for hands-on projects.

11:49 p.m.

Have I always tucked my arm under the pillow like this when I'm on my side? I guess for a while. Maybe I should do a sleep study like they did on *Mad About You*. Was it *Mad About You*? It was one of those shows from the 90s. If I did a sleep study, then I'd be able to see how much I move around. Maybe I don't need to know. Yeah, who needs to see that. I guess if I move around too much, someone at some point will tell me.

Yeah, if anyone's back in bed with me for long enough to have a problem with it!

There'll be someone to hate how much I move around in my sleep. I... think?

12:02 a.m.

I wonder what LA will be like? I'm only there for a few months but it will be the closest I've come to living there. I hope I'm productive. I think I will be. I'll have a space, and my schedule will be different. This voice-over project is exciting. I'm glad I'm making this a priority and will be there in person. I've never really recorded with the other actors, it's always in a booth by myself. It's not every day though. Not at all. I'll write on the other days, try to set up some other projects I've been thinking about. Maybe I'll be able to set aside some time to conquer a drawing project, maybe one small drawing every day? That would be awesome.

I'll never do that. There's no way.

Maybe a few drawings the whole time? Even that would be great. It would be so cool to have a show one day. I have to set a goal to have a small little gallery show somewhere with my work. What is my work even like now? It could be so many things. I'm still interested in some of the same themes as I was in college, but I wonder if my style has changed? I have to just do it already. Well, it'll be great when I do it. When I get some time, I'll go and buy some materials, some heavy board and colored pencils, and get to it. I'll do it, you'll see!

Who. The. Fuck. Are. You. Talking to???

12:15 a.m.

Fuck, Brainwaves has turned off.
Gotta reset it.
How am I still awake?
I will *NOT* be awake by the time this round ends. No sir!

12:44 a.m.

I hate that I made that wrong turn on the highway and it

became a whole fucking thing. How the silence spun into something it didn't need to. Why did I let that happen? Why didn't I just say something to her right then? Just said what I was feeling? She could have said something too though. I hardly *ever* make wrong turns, especially when I'm using my phone as a guide. I wonder how I did that? I guess I wasn't paying close enough attention and it had been a big weekend. I hate this moment, this memory. I should have forced myself to speak, to say that I cared, that I was there, that I was sorry—to say all the things we were really thinking about. I wish I would have had the courage I have now to ask what was going through her mind, how she was feeling. It wasn't about the wrong turn and I knew that. I knew that.

I need to move positions.

12:53 a.m.

I wonder what she's doing. I know she's not thinking about me, how could she be? She's moved on. I can't believe I'm still here, thinking about her, running through all this. Fuck. Stop doing this! What is wrong with me, why can't I stop replaying these scenes? I'm like a detective trying to uncover some clue that doesn't really matter. I'm so mad at myself. What did I think about before all this bullshit? I guess I was just sleeping before.

What a pathetic detective.
That'd be a good show. *The Pathetic Detective.* She sadly solves

crimes for other people dealing with heartache, finding the truth of the matter, one clue at a time.

She'd have a dope look though, sleek, tight leather pants and high boots that were comfortable enough to run in. An effortless top that looked like it was just thrown on with the pants. Piece-y hair with a bold lip. She'd slip in and out of parties, have a signature drink, a Dark and Stormy (also her signature demeanor), and get what she needed to close the case. But in the wee hours of the night she pores over her own unsolved case, rifling through her memory, playing back scenes for some clue, some resolution…that might never come. A loner, an introvert, a style icon (?)—she is, *The Pathetic Detective*.

1:15 a.m.

The red light from the TV is back. The washcloth must have slipped.
Just ignore it.
I can fall asleep with one tiny red light on in the room! It'd be crazy if I let this bother me! I'll just turn the other way.

No! I can't let it go.

I'll pee while I'm up, then it's not like I got up *just* to cover the stupid red light on the TV, it'll be like I had to pee and just happened to see the light!

Glad I got my alibi in order??? What? Just do what you need to do.

1:22 a.m.

Do I still have to pee?
No, it's okay.
I'll be able to go to sleep, I *just* peed. I'll just lie on my back.

Fuck me, I still have to pee.
I am the fucking worst.

1:30 a.m.

My shoulder is killing me—I'll just stretch my arm around in a circle.
This would all be on the sleep study video if I went into a center. I can't have this on tape, me doing arm circles in the middle of the night and cracking my wrist like a mad person.
Ohhhh, that was a good one, loud! The ache is still there, maybe crack it again?
Nothing.
Why does this wrist always ache? Maybe I've been bitten by a spider and instead of it giving me spidey-superpowers, it gave me a dull ache all the time? Or *maybe*, before the superpowers come out, they lie dormant in your body for years as a dull ache in your left wrist!?
Am I spider woman!?!?

1:46 a.m.

Brainwaves ended again. I can't believe it ended *again*.

Hmm. I guess I could check out this dating app for a sec while I'm up.
I hate that I'm on here so much. Why am I doing this?
I'm being proactive and putting myself out there!
Ugh, that's such bullshit, I look at videos of guys and girls and like no one. I'm not going to find someone on here.

I should stop with this, it makes me feel so shitty. I can't do this anymore. I should just stay on the road forever, this is where I belong. Alone in a car, moving from city to city, not able to be with anyone anyways! Because I'd never be in a place long enough—I'd have a built-in excuse!

That's not what I want.
Stop. Stop thinking about this because it is making me too sad.

I should delete this app right now off my phone. Yeah! I'm going to.
DE-LETE!
I will never put it on my phone again! I'm done! Real-life love connections await me!

2:10 a.m.

Maybe slow music instead of Brainwaves. Yeah, slow jams will lull me to sleep.

I have to find the right spot. I need to hug a pillow.

I'd kill in the dating scene if it was just pillows.

I'm never falling asleep.

I should really check out those sleep study centers, I think this is becoming a problem.

A — PIECE
with
ABBI JACOBSON
OF — WORK

WNYCSTUDIOS   MoMA

SHAMELESS   SELF PROMOTION

BEST BAGELS

Measuring one's life in bagels is no easy task. But like everything else, it's a way to see where you've been and where you're going, and possibly patterns in weight fluctuation. I haven't been eating many bagels lately—thus the influx of thoughts about bagels?? But I'm not worried, bagels and I have a well-trodden past, and I know we're in it for the long run.

The Bagel Factory

The first touch of freedom. In high school when I was a junior and senior, you could design your schedule in such a way that allowed you to leave school for lunch. Like a real adult, smack dab in the middle of the day, we had forty-five minutes to do as we pleased! One of the popular spots was The Bagel Factory, a local bagel shop, five minutes from school and the perfect food for the past version of myself that wore headscarves and operated at peak weed consumption. I don't remember if these bagels were particularly good, but those thirty-five minutes of freedom we had while eating them in those corner booths is something I'll always remember.

Sunday morning bagels

The most Jewish part about my overnight camp, beside the number of "steins," "baums," "sons," and "bergs" at the ends of last names, was the fact that every Sunday morning, they served bagels. The excitement over bagels was a weekly thing. This might say more about the rest of the food than it does about the bagels.

Famous 4th Street Delicatessen

In 2009, I ran the Philadelphia Half Marathon (not-so-humble brag), and afterward I went to Famous 4th Street Deli for a bagel and lox. Famous 4th is a classic Philly spot, but it was more the connection to the marathon that landed it on this list. I'd been training in Astoria on my own for months leading up to this run, particularly around the track in Astoria Park, underneath the Triborough Bridge. Before the race, I'd only ever run 8 miles at once, and 13.1 was a shit ton of miles for someone who doesn't consider themself a runner. But I wanted to do this, needed to challenge myself in this physical way. A few friends of mine were going to run the race with me, and all three of them ended up bowing out, so it was me, on my own, which is how I preferred it. I don't like running with anyone. People who can talk while exercising—anything more than a hike or walk—are insane to me. You want to tell me the drama that's currently going on at your office? Ohh, your co-worker plays their music too loud?? It's distracting and no one else seems to care?? I can't breathe right now! We're *running*, I'm just trying to stay alive! So, I was happy in the end to run it alone. Seeing the city from that point of view, running down the middle of Broad Street through Philadelphia, was unreal. It was beautiful and truly one of the hardest things I've willingly put myself through. I ran the whole way—my goal—although the pace got slower and slower, but I kept moving. The half marathon ended right in front of the art museum, and as I rounded the corner, the Rocky Balboa statue behind me, I felt like I could do anything I set my mind to, even if it was done very slowly and painfully. I limped to the car with my family and we went to Famous 4th Street Deli. That $16.50 (this is the actual price) humongous bagel and lox sandwich never tasted so good.

Brooklyn Bagel

Killing time. Brooklyn Bagel was a few blocks away from UCB Theatre in Chelsea, and it was a spot I'd go before classes or shows to elongate my anxiety and nervousness for what was about to happen. I filled notebooks with ideas and fears, sitting at those shitty, generic tables. The bagels here are so good, but huge. One is almost like eating two. Which at the time felt like quite the deal!

Bergen Bagels

Love is getting two different bagel sandwiches and splitting them on the grass in the shade, on a perfect day in Prospect Park. That's all I'll say about that.

"The Shore" bagels

A lot of Philly people go "down the shore" over the summer. It's the term they use to describe the many coastal towns in mostly southern New Jersey. My mom's parents had a house there and we'd spend any time that we weren't at camp down there with them. The air is different, salty and hot, but familiar. We'd ride bikes to pick up bagels in the morning when I was a kid, and now I go on walks with my mom to pick them up. Bagels are tradition down there, as thick as the accent.

The Hidden Bean bagels

This was a café I worked in Baltimore my freshman year of college, but even after I worked here it was my local spot. Every couple of Saturdays, MICA (the college I attended) provided a bus that would go up to New York City for the day. It would leave at 7 a.m. and return at around 9 p.m. This bus trip was precious to me and I never *ever* went with anyone. I remember feeling the awkwardness if someone I knew was on the bus as I boarded, how I'd have to explain that I had plans already, and that my plans were in fact having no plans at all. Other students would go on this trip together. They'd end up going to the museums, getting lunch, laughing and being the carefree newly minted nineteen-year-old adults they were. I'd stare out the bus window listening to music, chomping away on a cinnamon raisin bagel with butter I'd grabbed from the café for the ride. Soon I would step off the bus on my own, in the most interesting place in the whole world.

Yom Kippur bagels

My family manages to "fast" until around 4 p.m. We're terrible, but the bagels my dad gets are great.

Bacon, egg, and cheese

A bacon egg and cheese with Ilana, anywhere, anytime.

Bagel bites

Bagel bites were one of my brother's and my favorite dinners as a kid. Isn't this just a common truth for anyone who grew up in the '90s? We'd watch *Fresh Prince of Bel-Air*, and he'd get up and dance for my mom and me to the opening theme music in front of the TV.

Jack and Estelle's egg bagels

My grandparents, my dad's parents, were the only people I knew that loved egg bagels. It's all they bought, all they made us for breakfast when we slept at their apartment on City Line Avenue. I'd never pick an egg bagel, but that smell brings me right back to them.

JEROME, ARIZONA

On my way out of Arizona, toward California, I planned a very personal detour through Jerome. I had been there years before, on a trip with my dad and brother. We stopped for lunch on the way to Flagstaff where our journey through the Grand Canyon would begin. It was April of 2001, and I was seventeen, a junior in high school, and my dad pulled me out of class for ten days to go on a dory boat (small and wooden as opposed to a raft) trip down the Colorado River. My English teacher was not happy and almost failed me, because of my absence and my lack of involvement in the reading assignments relating to *The Crucible*. But what I took away from that trip far outweighed the by-rote education often taught in the public school system. I returned to school in time for us to NOT discuss any of the most important issues and allegories surrounding the play, but rather watch the 1996 movie incarnation starring Daniel Day-Lewis. I might have missed my teacher's stray observations on Arthur Miller's handiwork, but I had been on an adventure.

And now I was on another one, but this time I was going to Jerome for my mom.

My mom is unlike anyone I've ever met. Her capacity to love and thoughtfulness toward others have been through lines in her life. She is five foot one, with spiky hair, two hearing aids, and a cochlear implant, but her enthusiasm for life is roaring. It fills up any space she enters. She's reinvented her life over and over again, finding new love, new friends, new shells... She's been making a lot of shell art lately.

My mom lost her hearing when she was in her twenties. It was nerve damage, but there was never a specific cause or moment to pinpoint what happened. She hardly ever talks about it and doesn't allow anyone to feel bad for her. She isn't defined by her disability, in fact I have never even thought of her as having one. She's literally a bionic woman, a tiny superhero walking among us. We laugh when she does an Emily Litella (one of Gilda Radner's most famous characters), hearing a word or phrase *so* close to what was said, but in her interpretation, it's hilarious and doesn't totally make sense. The last time this happened, we had a whole conversation where I was talking about my childhood and the lack of Jews around, and she thought I'd been talking about the lack of *juice*! "What do you mean? We always had orange juice!" She's always able to laugh with it, but I know it affects her. She doesn't like crowded places because it's easier for her to miss parts of conversations and she worries about power outages and batteries being charged because she depends on them. It must have been so hard for her to lose her hearing right when life was picking up. For something so vital to be all of a sudden taken away like that and for life to just continue on.

I often wonder if her hearing loss is one of the reasons she began making more with her hands, leaning into the other senses because that one was failing her. Throughout my childhood, besides being a mom and working at Bed Bath & Beyond, she had a bunch of businesses that she ran out of our house. "Do Me a Favor" (best name ever?) was a party favor company where people could hire her to help plan their kids' birthday parties. There's a picture of us and my brother in a local newspaper, advertising the range of party favors and services available. She also had a clothing line she sold at craft shows, mostly consisting of vests and dresses she would paint and draw on—my personal favorite? Tie-vests (ties were sewn around the bottom of the entire circumference of a vest, so they hung and swung around when you walked). I used to wear one of these to school every so often—not the typical fourth-grader outfit, but she was never trying to make anything typical. Her shifting media and interests is something I find in my own work—the ability and desire to try new things is always there. When she moved to working with clay, my mom really found her voice; she combined her love of hand-building (without a pottery wheel) and found objects to make her clay boxes. They were all different sizes, and over the years, she experimented with style and changing the way she glazed and fired them. She started collecting antiques and objects, not just for our home, but now for her art—marbles, tiny dollhouse furniture, porcelain doll heads (these disembodied heads were terrifying)—and created scenes on the tops of the boxes. They were called "Boxes of Love," and each had a tiny piece of paper inside, with a message she'd seen somewhere and been inspired by that read:

BOX OF LOVE

*I bet you think this box is empty—it's not, it's full of love.
It's a very small box because there isn't one large enough to
hold all the Love I have to give. The wonderful thing is—I
didn't buy this LOVE—I was born with it and I can give it
to anyone I want. I hope you will enjoy and treasure my Love
because it never runs out and I have more to give.

*please don't sue my mom if you wrote this or know who
did. Consider it a loving homage.*

She became a fixture at craft shows in Philadelphia and New
Jersey and it's what we did on a lot of weekends when I was
a kid. My dad and her would set up this stand made from
wire shelving and we'd help her package her boxes with bubble wrap and bag them as they got sold, handing them happily
over to her customers. One weekend when I was about seven
or eight, she set up at the Garden State Racetrack in Jersey,
and I set up my own "booth," a tiny TV table next to her,
and sold football pencils for twenty-five cents a pop. Football
pencils, you ask? Yes, football pencils—pencils with team logos
and colors for NFL teams. I had been working at the school
store a few mornings before classes started, and saw that these
pencils were popular, so even though I knew nothing about
football or the teams (I was more of a soccer gal), I bought
them in bulk from the school store and sold them out of an
old tin box my grandfather gave me at the racetrack. I might
not have known much about football, but I was trained from a
young age to know what buying something wholesale and sell-

ing it for more meant. As often as people question my Judaism, I should probably lead with this fact. I organized the pencils and got everything ready—I had change on hand and rubber bands if people bought a bunch. I had been watching my mom run her business for years, I couldn't share a booth with her and not make some sales! I'm guessing it was refreshing to see a small, scrappy tomboy pushing her favorite-color-football pencils rather than your typical paper cup of lemonade. The business folded shortly after, as I moved on to more important things like socializing, but I made all my money back, plus some, like a proper Forbes under 10.

Regardless of my own thriving football pencil corporation, it was incredible to see that drive and creativity from my mom's work come to fruition—to watch her process of finding those objects, building the boxes with her hands in our basement, and then selling them to people who were most likely going to give them to someone else as gifts. It wasn't making her rich, but it brought so much joy to her and her customers—to have a thing she made from nothing except her hands and heart move through the world like that. I am continually trying to find that in my own work. Watching her allowed me to see how objects can and should have significance, about the importance of paying attention to detail. That the small things matter: the materials, the service, the setup, the follow-through, the face-to-face, and most important, the drive you had to make the thing in the first place. The better she got, and the more she found her voice through pottery, the more confident she became. She took risks and tried new things, always reinventing her creativity, always curious. The boxes became hand mirrors, which became sculptures; she started doing collages and murals on the walls of our basement with found objects. And now of course...the shells. There's always something else to be excited about.

My mom had first discovered Jerome when I was in high school, on a trip with her boyfriend, Don. On my drive down from Sedona, I started to think about my teen years, that brief time that seems to hold an uneven amount of power over the rest of my life. When my parents first started dating new people after their divorce, believe it or not, I *wasn't* excited about it. I was just starting to come to terms with my somewhat nomadic lifestyle—my brother had gone off to college, so from thirteen on, it was just me (and our pug, Luke) moving from my mom's house to my dad's house and vice versa, every Sunday night, all while managing the various confusions of daily life as an up-and-coming adult. I didn't have time to deal with the fact that my parents were moving on and falling in love with new people, I had enough on my plate!

Things I was preoccupied with during my teen years:

How to not cough every time I smoked weed

How much of a flare my jeans should have

The concept of flirting

How to manage my frizzy hair, and which headscarf I should wrap it in

Finding the most unique black light poster to go with the black light I got in my room at my dad's house (without a poster, the black light only served to reveal prior tenants' stains on the carpet)

Trying not to think about what specifically the stains on my carpet were

All of the sexual firsts—doing them, how to do them, with who, where to do them...

Taking advantage of this new freedom of being able to drive myself places

Constantly trying to find some part of my body to be okay with

Seeing for myself what this Atkins craze was all about, and determining how much cheese was too much

Maintaining a solid B average

Where I was going to go to college

What college was going to be like

SATs, and if it was okay to take them without taking an SAT prep class

Trying to hide the fact that every friend of mine was taking an SAT prep class from my parents

How far was too far for me and my friends to drive to see basically *any* jam band play live

Being socially active, in real life by day, and on top of AOL chat rooms and instant messages by night

How to play indoor soccer well, after I discovered marijuana

Relying on potato chips for pain relief of menstrual cramps

What it was like to have this new, portable phone that I was supposed to carry around at all times

How to avoid getting caught drinking

How to avoid getting caught smoking pot

How to avoid getting caught hooking up with someone

How to avoid getting caught throwing a party at one parent's house when they were away and I was supposed to be staying at the other one

So many important, worldly concerns to maintain and stay on top of—I didn't have spare time to process how I felt about real, emotional developments happening at home! Do you know how hard it is to cover up and completely forget about stains on a fully carpeted bedroom floor? Just the sight of the black light, hanging on the wall above my closet, not even lit up, made me remember the stains.

I was purposefully not thinking about my parents' divorce, and how different my life was. But it was more difficult now, their new partners were unavoidable, new people in my life, out at dinners, trying to get to know me by asking about how school was going. *School is fine.* I didn't want or expect my parents to get back together, but I didn't want or know how to talk or deal with these new people.

My mom dated Don for most of the time I was in high school. He was from Kentucky, and wore cowboy boots and had a big mustache like Tom Selleck. My mom is an antiques collector and they met at his antiques store a few towns over. He was sweet and caring and treated my mom like a queen. I remember they went on a vacation to Europe and her face lit up as she told me every detail down to the baroque twists in the metal railing on their hotel room balcony. She was smitten. I was happy for her, because I knew how difficult the divorce had been—my parents had been together for over twenty-five years. They met at overnight camp when they were fifteen and got married when they were twenty. They had my brother at twenty-six and me at twenty-nine, and they got divorced when they were in their mid-forties. Even at seventeen, I could see how they'd each changed, how her and my dad didn't fit anymore. But understanding why the divorce happened didn't make the fact that new people were in my life any easier. Don really fucking tried though; he'd cook us breakfast—scrambled eggs with these potatoes from a can—which sounds pretty terrible, but they were amazing, one of those unexpectedly delicious dishes you forever associate with someone, and are never able to replicate the flavors. He offered me side jobs raking his yard, and every Christmas, he'd pay me by the hour to wrap all the cookie tins he'd send out as gifts to everyone that worked at his company. We'd stack piles and piles of tins (there had to be over a hundred) in our living room, and I'd wrap them after school and on the weekend. It was one of the best jobs I've ever had. It made me the talented gift wrapper I am today.

Despite Don being so generous and lovely, I didn't give him much back. I was just sort of "fine." I was friendly at times, but I don't think I was ever really, completely myself. I couldn't fake it. I know Don wasn't sure how I felt about him, probably because *I* wasn't sure. I wasn't sure about his cowboy boots or hats. I didn't know how I felt about his mustache or him being at dinners all the time or any of it. I was at my mom's house for one week, and now he was there too? It was the same at my dad's house, with his girlfriend. Could I get some space?! I have to figure out how to stop coughing every time I smoke this weed, and the more adults there are in the house, the harder this is going to be! It obviously wasn't just that—it was space in general. My life had just changed so drastically, I wanted everything to slow down or for my *own* life to pick up.

You know when you look back on specific moments—I'm talking the big, bad ones that stay with you forever, the ones you push down and don't think about until you drive across the country to a specific tiny town, situated on the top of a hill—how you wish you had been more mature, more equipped with the words and actions and vulnerability to deal with those things? How you wish you could have been more loving, and gentle and kind. I'm not sure what to do with those moments.

Don died suddenly in October of 2001, of an aortic aneurysm. When I think of that night, it plays like a movie, scene after scene, scored by the random mix CD playing in my Jeep Wrangler as I drove home from the hospital in the middle of the night to my dad's house after my mom told me I should go. Even in that moment, sitting in the waiting room after the doctor gave us almost zero hope, she was being a mom. It was late, and scary, and I don't think she wanted me to see what she was about to. I should have stayed with her.

A month after Don died, I went to visit colleges in New England. I was supposed to go with my friend Mary and her dad the day after he died, but my plan changed, obviously, so my dad ended up taking me a month later. We also took my mom. This just felt right. Weird, but right. I didn't end up going to any of the schools we visited on that trip, but this adventure with my parents was necessary. That month had been so unwieldy. 9/11 had just happened, and then Don. I was supposed to pick a college and leave home and start the rest of my life. There was nothing to grasp onto, only trying to move forward. I never even processed what a bizarre situation that was: a two-day road trip with the people who made me, a month after my mom's partner had died suddenly, or the fact that I hadn't been alone with my parents for this long in over five years. But it was like we hadn't skipped a beat—my dad drove my mom's car as we sang along to oldies. We shared food at restaurants, we navigated (with a *paper* map!) together, my dad did bits through the connecting door of our hotel rooms. My mom laughed again. It was like we'd somehow figured out how to time-travel. It was a much-needed distraction for her, being with my dad, the person who knew her best, during the time that might have been her worst.

The resilience my mom showed in bouncing back from Don dying is astounding to me. Especially now as I find myself on the last leg of a road trip trying to get over my own broken heart. Pain shouldn't be quantified or compared, but I can't even imagine how much pain she must have been in. If I'm depressed and can't seem to get back to normal from *this bullshit* (it's not bullshit, but you know what I mean)—how must she have felt? However my mom felt, and still feels from that time in her life, she somehow moved through it. She always has.

Don and my mom had loved Sedona, but even more, they *loved* Jerome. It was a tiny town they discovered while on vacation, one they talked about so much it felt like it was only theirs. They were both antiques collectors, filling their weekends with early-morning flea markets and estate sales, so stumbling upon Jerome was like opening a treasure chest full of weird eccentrics and southwestern art. Even bringing up Jerome makes my mom joyous. She has a painting of the steep main street hanging in her house right now. It's one of her favorite things.

The Christmas after Don died, my mom presented me with a ring that he'd bought me in Jerome. He planned on giving it to me then. My mom put it in an antique ring box and hung it up on our Christmas tree (I am 100 percent Jewish) as an ornament for me to open last. It's a gold band, with a flower on the top, an opal in the center with turquoise stones surrounding it. I wore that ring all through senior year of high school, every day of college, and throughout my twenties in New York City. Wearing that ring felt like a connection to him, the only way for me to show I cared, to apologize for being an angsty teenager who never gave him the time of day. When *Broad City* got picked up, I decided to give the ring to my character. Getting to make a television show was unbelievable, but also *very* scary. I knew I'd feel better wearing his ring—whenever I got nervous or felt insecure or scared, the ring was my amulet, always right there with me. It is the one thing my character *has* to have on, the one thing the entire wardrobe department knows means the world to me. The significance behind that ring is so big, so heavy, like a Pandora's box of my adolescence I don't choose to open often, but the sight of it is enough, a Cliffs-Notes version of my past, a headline of where I've been.

So, I went to Jerome. I ate eggs and toast at the counter of a tiny café on the main drag, in one of the buildings on that steep street in my mom's painting. I thought of my mom, her courage and her enthusiasm. I thought of Don and his cowboy boots and his mustache, his ring, and that time in my life. I thought of my parents and that trip we took all those years ago. I thought about how pain can usually means change. I thought about bouncing back. How we can start again. And again.

WHEN AND WHERE

It's unbelievable how happy my ex-girlfriend is.

There isn't anyone happier in the history of people or happiness. It's a modern miracle. Her day-to-day is jam-packed with boundless joy and she's never felt more fulfilled or satisfied in her whole life. She dances to places instead of walking. Her face hurts from smiling, every coin she sees on the street is faceup, and she gets TRIPLE punches on her coffee punch card, every time, no matter who is the cashier that day. She's fucking all the hottest, smartest, funniest people, and they're doing stuff in bed I haven't even heard of! She's keeping all her plants alive and not only that, flowers are blooming out of plants that don't even grow flowers. She's moved on in a way that has somehow deleted any trace of our relationship, and found herself in a land of abundance, chock-full of perfect dates and new romantic adventures. It's astounding how well she's doing. I can't believe it. And not only in love, but also with work, with friends, intimacy, fashion, even bagels—there isn't one area of her life that hasn't been improved since we dated.

It's not that I'm not happy, don't get me wrong, but I'm not happy at all. The difference in our happiness is extremely large. If I had an appropriate state or "big thing" to compare this "large" difference with, like Texas or some sort of prizewinning gourd compared with a normal-size gourd, I would, but numbers and state sizes and farming statistics weren't ever something I excelled at. I try and stick to what I know. With that said, you can only imagine what it'd be like for me to run into her. It'd be interesting for sure. As I drive closer to Los Angeles, the city I know she's in, the thought of the inevitable chance encounter brings a steady trickle of anxiety throughout my body. The fact that she and I haven't talked in months and my main news source about her heavenly life post-me happens to be the deepest, darkest parts of my brain and heart makes my mind spin. I could see her anywhere. ANYWHERE.

What if I'm in a bookstore and I see her? What if I've been there awhile at this point. I *was* browsing the cool aisles, filled with memoirs and short-story collections. I picked up some of the employee suggestions, rifled through a few art criticism essays. I was over there for so long, in *those* aisles. But what if when I see her I am holding a book by Guy Fieri? What if I remembered I had to get a gift and I picked that book up and thought, *Hey, this would be a perfect book for the person I need a gift for,* just as she walked in. What would I say then? I don't hate Guy Fieri, but I would want to tell her that I was *actually* interested in so *many* other books in the store, and if it was up to me, if I didn't need to get this fucking gift at this fucking moment, that I'd instead be holding a stack of Raymond

Carver and Rebecca Solnit and other notable writers that make me think about life and not tacos or root beer floats. I like tacos, sure, but this trip wasn't about that initially. I've never had a root beer float, but that's another story altogether. I couldn't say any of that. So, here I am.

What if I'm walking past a string of shops, and I happen to peek into a salon and see a woman getting her hair cut inside? The haircut is incredible, one of those short-but-not-too-short, wavy-but-not-too-wavy, messy cuts that you look at and are immediately jealous of. I realize I haven't had my hair cut in a while, and I could use a change, so I go in and ask for exactly the same haircut as the woman before me—if she can pull it off, I sure as hell can! I'm a modern woman! I sit in the chair and smile as my damp hair is combed and cut. I read a five-year-old *Glamour* magazine, pondering how "women really can do it all," when an employee slips on the freshly mopped floor (that he just mopped!) and falls into my hairdresser, making him slip and cut a huge chunk of my hair off. It's a wreck and there's no going back. There's just NO way this cut can be salvaged. So, I leave. They don't charge me of course, that would be absurd, though I'd probably pay if they didn't insist. The mopper slipped and sprained his ankle for crying out loud. My hairstylist was mortified and got a small cut on his pinky finger from the incident. He might not be able to work tomorrow, it's his cutting hand. "It's just hair," I say, "it'll grow back." I feel good about being so kind and forgiving. Maybe this was a lesson—outward appearances aren't the most important thing. It's inner beauty that matters. I leave the salon, waving and smiling. They look at me, their eyes all silently say, *Wow, what a generous soul*, and *I wish I could be more like her*. What if at that moment on the sidewalk outside the salon, *she* walks by? We haven't seen each other in months and here I am looking like I have a ripped piece of construction paper, bouncing on top of my head. There'd be no way to convey the series of events that just occurred. It wouldn't be appropriate for me to pull someone out of the salon to back up my story. She'd think I *chose* this haircut, was smiling about it! I couldn't correct her, explaining that I was smiling about how kind I was, how forgiving. Oh, boy. I couldn't tell her about the freshly mopped floor or the cut pinky finger, or that I wanted to pay. Could you even imagine if that was where I saw her? That'd be a mess for sure.

What if I'm dressed up to go to a wedding? I happen to be a bridesmaid, like I am sometimes when I go to weddings. Not all the time, obviously, but sometimes I am a bridesmaid. What if I'm wearing a pastel-purple bridesmaid dress, a dress selected for me? A dress from a bridal shop that only sells dresses just like this, in pastel purple or ochre or grass green—dresses that will be worn one time and then hang in a closet as a distant memory, reminding us of that night. Forever a relic of the mismatched grouping of girls brought together by the bride. The awkward forced bonding of people who don't know each other. A bridesmaid's dress cannot be thrown away or donated. If the bride comes over, this dress must be hanging in the closet. What if she looks through my closet while I'm in the bathroom or out back and the dress isn't there? I'd have to get an "out back" of course. I imagine one day I'll have one though and I could be out there pruning the flowers or something and the bride would be over for dinner and find herself in my closet, and if the dress isn't in there, it could be bad. I'd have to lie right there on the spot, out back. If I'm going to have an "out back," I don't want to have to lie out there. So, what if I'm wearing that dress on the way to the wedding and I see *her*? I'm with the bride, so I can't stop and explain the whole dress situation. I can't say how I didn't pick it and that it isn't my new style. I couldn't mention anything about the asymmetric neckline and how I was the last bridesmaid asked to be in the wedding, thus getting the last choice in necklines. I'm not gonna say that right in front of the bride. It's also totally fine—we'd lost touch, the bride and me, but I care about our friendship, so I'm happy to be a part of her big day. I think it would be clear that I'm in a pastel-purple asymmetrical dress for the wedding. She'd see the bride and get it, right? I mean, she would probably put two and two together. But who knows? Dresses are complicated and who knows. What then?

What if I see her and it's pouring? I didn't bring an umbrella because I'm not in New York City, and I've stopped carrying umbrellas since I left. In New York I was so good about bringing an umbrella if the Weather Channel app on my phone said it might rain later that day. Even if the chances were slim, I'd bring one. You never know. But I'm not in New York City and things are different in my life, including weather. What if it just starts pouring when I see her? What if we're outside on the street, and neither of us has an umbrella and so we have to run away to our cars. Would I yell out that I'm not running away because of her, but because of the rain? I would hope she would hear it clearly enough to understand. That's a lot to yell, especially when it's raining.

What if I'm mid-conversation with a friend when I see her? It happens to be a serious conversation and I am being an attentive friend. Listening and nodding, and occasionally offering up some insightful piece of advice about open communication. I've been working a lot on communication for myself, and this friend's issue happens to be in that department. It's weird when things line up like that—a weakness you've been working on personally gets shined back at you through someone else's issue. Wow, what a coincidence. But this friend needs me, and I am there, solid and nurturing. What if I see *her* right then in the middle of that? Then what? A good friend would just keep going, keep nurturing. Friendship is hard to find and I want my friends to know I care and support them, unconditionally. But what if she's just there all of a sudden. What if my friend is crying when I see her! Then what? I could try and silently motion with one arm. (The friend is leaning on me, weighing down my other arm so I can't lift it—it's fallen asleep actually, which is a whole other situation. Lately things have been falling asleep—limbs and extremities that is. I should probably see someone about it. My friend doesn't need to hear about it right now though, that's for sure. I can tell them later, get their advice, see if they know any specialists.) Anyway, I guess I could gesture to her with my one free arm that *I can't right now, my friend needs me.* I could try and mouth the words, *I'm sorry, I'm a good friend, and I'm being supportive and sharing my newfound but limited knowledge regarding communication.* But those things are hard to understand unless you can read lips. I don't think she can. It wasn't ever something she seemed interested in, but who knows? Maybe she can now. I can only hope.

What if I see her after a fitness class? I have been working out more and this particular class is extremely intense. It's seventy-five minutes. I can't believe I made it through. What if I see her in the parking lot after that class, and I'm drenched in sweat? I can't explain how long the class was, or how challenging it is. Who does that? I'm getting better since I started taking the class and can almost muster up the courage to attempt to do a headstand. I can't brag about that to her. You can't just begin a casual discussion with where you're at in terms of headstands. It's a longer conversation. So, I'm just dripping sweat and my shirt is wet and I can't explain any of it! Some people even bring an extra shirt to change into after class because they're so sweaty, so I'm not the only one, but I didn't bring an extra shirt, because as much as I try to plan my life anticipating disaster, bringing an extra shirt never seemed dire. Now I know. Then there's the whole ordeal of me standing there in workout clothes and sandals. And not cool sport sandals. They're really cute sandals, ones I'd wear with jeans. *Extremely* cute actually. But with yoga clothes, what am I thinking? She'd probably be wondering why I'm not in sneakers. She'd probably think this is how I dress now. She'll think I wear workout clothes as regular clothes during the middle of the day with cute sandals. I could find a car or something to walk behind, hiding my bottom half. No, too much time has already gone by. She'd know about the sandals. It'd be over as soon as it began.

What if I see her in line for a bathroom at a Starbucks? I had to pee so badly, and so I stopped inside a Starbucks. I'd then do what I always do: act like I'm going to get in line to buy a coffee and spontaneously realize I have to pee, and then, again, I spontaneously come up with the solution to pee first and then buy the coffee. The silent play I enacted seemed to convey my whole plan to the baristas, so I felt okay going to get in line for the bathroom. What if I'm waiting and the person in the bathroom I'm waiting for is taking so long. The line is building behind me. Finally, they leave the bathroom. What if it's *her* leaving the bathroom? Not to say she was taking so long because she was taking a massive dump. That's not what I was saying. I think she'd actually be putting lipstick on and fixing her hair and that's why she was taking so long. Maybe some-one texted her and she responded while still in the bathroom. That's probably why she was in there so long. What would I say as she opened the bathroom door with a paper towel so as not to touch the doorknob? I couldn't say much. The line is so big behind me, I'd feel pressure to go in. I'd get inside and lock the door, then I probably wouldn't even be able to pee because I just saw her. I'd come out and buy a coffee because I silently promised the baristas I would. I'd still have to pee so bad. I guess I could drive to another Starbucks.

What if I'm mid-bite at a restaurant, eating a new meal that I'm not used to. When you eat stuff you're used to, you know how the bites are gonna go. You have expectations, you can foresee dilemmas by having water or extra napkins handy. But sometimes when you're in a new situation (with a new sand-wich or something), things don't go as planned. Stuff falls out of your mouth, sometimes onto your clothes or the table, and what if that happens right when I see her. How will I play that out? Would I just laugh and clean up my mess like a rookie who clearly doesn't know how to deal with a new type of sandwich? Geez. You can't blame that kind of thing on the restaurant. No. Also, what if I like the new sandwich? You can't blame that type of situation on a new sandwich.

What if I decided to take scuba-diving lessons—you know, the ones they do in a swimming pool so you can get the feel for what it's like to breathe underwater? I signed up without even having an upcoming trip. I've been trying to sign up for more things, experience new environments, and be of the world a bit more. Those classes can be exciting even without the trip, right? I've also never seen the bottom of a pool that up close. I bet it's an experience in and of itself. What if I did that, signed up and bought a cool retro bathing suit, like the ones they have out now? Retro stuff seems to be back in all ways, especially bathing suits. So, what if I'm there, in the pool learning to scuba dive, and while I'm getting the hang of it—the whole breathing-underwater thing—I see her. She is at the bottom of the pool, too, and she's also getting the hang of breathing underwater. She was always good at getting the hang of things. She'd probably have a trip planned, though. Would I make up a whole trip down there? That's a lot to lie about down there at the bottom of the pool.

What if I saw her while I was making some sort of speech? I was up on a platform talking to an audience about something I was passionate about and she walked in. What if there were hors d'oeuvres in the back of the room and she was hungry? Maybe she was at the event, speaking about something she was passionate about, too. You'd think I would have seen some sort of flyer with both our names on it, or at least be informed of the other speakers so I knew where I stood. What kind of event is this, they don't even tell you what else is happening? Completely unprofessional. This is the perfect example of why I have to say no more often. Anyway, she was done for the day and before she left she got hungry, so she stumbled into the room where I was giving my speech to see what food was in there. Maybe the room where she gave her passionate speech didn't have any good food. Only those terrible hors d'oeuvres that make you wish there was no food at all, like rolled-up cold cuts or apple slices that have browned from sitting out too long. What if she walked in right as I was flipping over a piece of paper, so I wasn't even saying anything particularly good. It would appear like I was standing there, not speaking at all. This speech is great, don't get me wrong, but every once in a while, you have to flip over the piece of paper, or take a breath, and pause before you start to ramp up the passion. So, what if she walked in right when the ramp-up was starting? No one was applauding yet, or tearing up, nothing. What if she walked in and picked up some raw carrots (the fancy purple and yellow ones) and a pigs in a blanket (my room has a solid selection for vegetarians and meat eaters) and then just walked out and didn't even see it was me in there! I don't know how I'd continue ramping up if that happened.

What if I was singing karaoke and I saw her? I was up on a little stage, reading the lyrics, and she came into the bar right then. You can't get down off the stage mid-song when you're singing karaoke! I'd have to keep going. I don't think my voice is that good, but if she walked in right then, I would have to really bring it. I've never fully been able to "sing from my diaphragm," but I'd have to for sure in this situation. That would be a big night, and people would probably be blown away at my voice. Who knows what could happen from a night like that. Not to say that singing scouts go to karaoke clubs, but they might go just as patrons. One could be there that night where I'd have to sing my heart out because she was there. A scout could definitely be there and then who knows. Wow. What a night.

What if I decide to get Lasik eye surgery and I'm on my way home and I see her. Or rather the person guiding me home tells me she's there, on the street. I'm hobbling along, arm in arm with this amazing friend of mine who's helping me get home from surgery because you need assistance, and there she is. I'm wearing those bug-eye glasses they give you and she's there. What if she's there and I can't even see her? I always thought that when I ran into her, I'd be able to *see* her. I should have thought this out, but I had a lot on my mind. Lasik is VERY intense. You have to have your eyes open and you see the whole thing—because it's being done to your eyes. That might sound obvious, but think about it. I guess I could bring that up to her, the eyes-being-open thing. I just find it incredible that they slice your eye like that and you have no choice but to watch the whole thing! She'd probably know all about it already.

What if I took up Rollerblading? I feel like that's a thing that comes back every few years and what if I decided it's my year to take up Rollerblading. I would be out, blading, with those kneepads, elbow pads, and the weird, hard hand pads that are supposed to break your fall. I would be picking it up again. I was pretty athletic as a kid, it's not that surprising that

I'd be getting quick to pick it up again. What if I was blading and I felt it was time to take a risk and go down a steady incline. Everyone knows hills are the hardest and I'm not going to get into Rollerblading and not challenge myself. What would be the point of that? So, what if I'm going down the hill, wind in my face, and I'm actually doing it and what if I see her then, right there on the hill? I'd probably go right past her as I don't feel comfortable with the back-stopper brake yet, and I'm certainly not going to try and hockey-stop right there in the middle of the steady downward incline. What then? She'd see me go by and think I wasn't stopping even to say hello. I wouldn't be able to explain that even though I am athletic, I haven't really gotten the hang of stopping while going down a steady incline. I couldn't go into how it's way harder than it looks, or start talking about how some of the things we did as kids were so much easier because we weren't really scared of anything. I couldn't talk about how as adults we are so scared of everything. I couldn't say any of that. It wouldn't be good, obviously.

What if I am walking down the street—one of those streets out here that you drive to, just to walk around? There aren't a lot of those in Los Angeles, because people don't walk as much, so those streets are rare and hard to park on. So, what if one day I circle around and I get a good spot that I'm pretty excited about. Maybe even overly excited about. A good spot is something that can really change the course of your day. Entire energy patterns can be traced back to good spots out here. So, I'm walking around, browsing the various stores on this street, and I catch myself in the reflection in a store window. I think,

Wow, I look pretty good! And I do. I look very good. Effortlessly good. My hair is finally falling in a way I've always wanted. I have a style. I feel great, actually. I'm starting to feel good being out here in this new place and today is looking up. I like who I am. I'm walking and living and not thinking about the stressful things I usually think about. And then she's there, walking on the same sidewalk, doing the same thing. Nothing is going wrong. I am just standing there with her. It's like I've been standing there forever, not saying a word. I look at her, because I can't do much else. "Hi," she says.

BREATHE ME

...FUCK

PALM SPRINGS

I might have hallucinated and caught a glimpse of a sixty-year-old version of myself, swimming laps through a pool of people. I'm not positive, but it's possible.

It was one of the hottest days of the summer, at least for me. I was only in Palm Springs for one night, but the heat was so jarring, I couldn't imagine doing anything except going down to the pool. A public pool is a place I'm not usually itching to hang out at alone, as being solo usually means you're either a creep or asking to be talked to, but it was so disgusting outside I didn't care. The pool was packed even though it was a weekday, apparently everyone had the same idea. I tried to avoid going into the overly populated pool as long as I could, imagining the number of germs that might be in store, and convincing myself the mere proximity to water, the sight of splashing, would cool me down. But reading my book on a lounge chair under an umbrella was only making me hotter. Touching the fabric of the chair, the towel, wearing any clothing, basically *anything* at this point was unacceptable except the cool, refreshing water. I'd drink an Emergen-C and pop a B12 vitamin later, but for now, I was going in.

I found a spot next to the wall of the pool and hung off of it, spreading out my arms, people watching. Pockets of friends gathered in circles, drinking and laughing, enjoying the day. Families clustered together, kids played with toys and threw balls back and forth. I watched a couple, two women clearly in love, playing with their small dog. And that's when I saw it—a woman slowly stepped in and attempted to swim directly through the center of the pool, through all these people. She was probably in her mid-sixties, and wore goggles and a swim cap. She swam lengthwise, back and forth, stopping and restarting each time she swam into someone. If I haven't explained this in enough detail, I will do so again: It was over one hundred degrees in Palm Springs, in late July, and the Ace Hotel pool was packed with people trying to beat the heat, and then a woman in her sixties started doing laps through the middle of said packed pool. I could not believe what was happening.

I couldn't stop watching this feat, and I had so many questions. Why would she be attempting this during peak hours at a hotel pool? It seemed insane or useless, she couldn't swim too far without being interrupted by another person. Was this her daily routine, were *we* in the middle of *her* space, and not her trying to fight her way through ours? Was this a dare? Was she completely unaware or had she just stopped caring at all about what anyone thought of her? I was both emboldened and depressed by what I was watching: a simultaneous revolutionary show of autonomy and a delirious detachment from the world.

I felt like I was there to take witness. To see this moment, this woman and her afternoon laps. But no one else at the pool seemed to even notice her, even though she was physically bumping into them. I felt connected to her, felt *for* her. And that's when it occurred to me—*no one else was even noticing her?* No one else seemed to be as enthralled by this wonder woman. Also, no one seemed to notice *me*, watching *them*. Holy shit, this sauna-like heat was affecting more than just my sweat glands—was I hallucinating some sort of *Christmas Carol* situation where I was being presented with another version of myself, my future self?

It's quite a leap, as I don't swim laps that much—but maybe I'll start in my forties when I have access to a pool? Maybe in my sixties I'll re-create this road trip I'm on right now, and this is my last night on *that* road trip. Has *this* road trip been so meaningful—so significant that my future self yearns to repeat it, play by play? I guess it's nice to know I still stay in shape in my sixties.

Let's just say, for a moment, she is me. I couldn't really see her face with the goggles and the swim cap covering her/my hair, but let's just think of her as me. I'm the courageous swimmer daring to do laps in the middle of a chaotic world (pool). If that is me in thirty years, I hope these things are true:

I hope that I'm content, that there isn't anger within those freestyle strokes.

I hope I'm swimming for pleasure and health and not for some societal norm I'm trying to keep up with like pant size.

I hope my life is full of joy, full of adventure, full of love.

I hope I'm able to share my life with someone, with others.

I hope I'm comfortable in that bathing suit. Good ones are hard to find.

I hope I like myself, my choices, my gut instincts.

I hope I'm a member of the community, and take part in making the world I and others live in, better.

I hope I'm fulfilled creatively.

I hope I still have a voice, a platform, a medium in which to express myself.

I hope I'm fucking a ton of people, or one person, a ton.

I hope I don't care what other people think of me.

She's not me, I'm not her. We will go our separate ways and I will probably never encounter her again, but the way in which I see myself in her, or in regard to her, intrigues me. I've been driving across the country by myself trying to figure out who exactly I might be and what I really want, and then this woman just swims right through the fucking pool. Maybe we never fully figure it out. Maybe it keeps changing. Sometimes we're the swimmer, sometimes the one being swam into. Sometimes we're the one watching the whole thing in awe and confusion. Sometimes you have to get out of the pool because you're not wearing enough sunscreen and you just want to sit in your air-conditioned hotel room, watch terrible DIY renovations on TV, and order room service.

Folklore says if you're lucky, you'll catch a glimpse of her, going back and forth through the Palm Springs Ace Hotel pool—the lone swimmer—on an endless mission to boldly proclaim her self-determination, her independence, her way. Her forever drive toward feeling okay with who she is. They say if you see her, it's an omen.

At least I've got that going for me.

ACTUAL ALBUM COVER IS WAY MORE ELABORATE

ALL THE INCREDIBLE THINGS
I DID NOT DO

When you tell people you are going somewhere, whether it's a far-off destination, a weekend away in nature, or a restaurant downtown, you will most likely be inundated with the things you *must* do, *have* to see, *cannot* miss. Real life is like a constant Yelp review, everyone has notes on how the experience could be improved. As I planned my road trip I contemplated the best route to take, should I go north, and see the Badlands and the big sky in Montana? Drive the famous Route 66 across the Midwest? Or should I go south and hit up the Southwest and possibly the Grand Canyon? All ways seemed incredible, but when I shared my dilemma with others, every single person had an opinion, to a point where they all canceled each other out. I felt pressure, as if the drive would be a complete waste of time if I didn't cross all those things off my list and report back about my findings.

It was too much. Who was I going on this trip for? I just wanted to be, without the stress of a to-do list. So, I threw it out. I didn't do most of the things I was supposed to. I didn't dine at any of the places people raved about; I didn't eat BBQ in Nashville, or anywhere for that matter. I didn't go to Graceland like I thought I would. I didn't go to B.B. King's infamous club on the main drag in Memphis and hear blues, or see the fireworks display on the roof of the fancy hotel in the center of town. I didn't see the bats fly out from under the bridge as night fell in Austin, or do laps in Barton Springs. I didn't buy peaches on the side of the road on my way to far-West Texas, or stop in any of the antiques stores lining route 10 through Fredericksburg. I didn't go to the Judd or the Chianti Foundations, or see hardly any of the art in the far-flung reaches of the desert. I didn't go to Big Bend or stop at the Carlsbad Bat Caves. I didn't visit Georgia O'Keeffe's house in Abiquiu like I planned. I didn't see Bear's Ears or go canyoneering in Zion. I didn't do any drugs or fuck any strangers. I didn't go to any concerts or secret back-bar hotspots, and the only dance parties I attended were the solo ones inside my hotel rooms and driver's seat.

Maybe that means I missed out on the most coveted places these cities and destinations have to offer, but I found my own way. I found what I needed. I went to bad bars and biked around town. I drove in circles and got pissed about parking and ate at Whole Foods in Nashville. I bought fried green tomatoes from a greasy pub, got soaked in the rain and watched *The West Wing* in my hotel room in Memphis. I got tacos from a truck in Marfa, read on a foldout chair in the parking lot and spent time with people I knew in my gut would become important to me. I wandered. It was a mess and not perfect and all mine. I got lost, and that's okay.

It's okay to not see all the art and not meet all the locals and not walk all the famous walks or hear all the indie bands in the coolest venues in town. It's okay to go to sleep early and spend too long finding the good coffee spot but not seeing the historical sights. It's okay. It's okay to not figure it all out. It's okay to feel broken and alone and scared sometimes. It's okay to not know everything. It's okay to not eat where everyone tells you to, or not take a selfie in front of everything you've seen or done and post on the internet for friends and strangers to see. It's okay to go away and come back. It's okay. It's okay if it's not all amazing or incredible or spectacular. It's okay. It's okay to leave earlier than you expected, to drink too much or not drink at all. It's okay to replay stupid moments you regret in your mind and it's okay to not have moved on completely. It's okay to be fucking pissed. Everyone is on their own timeline when it comes to love, so it's okay. It's okay to think it's not okay. It's okay to go off the grid and not be in touch. It's okay to take a second and to breathe and to cry. It's okay to be tender. It's okay to fail. It's okay to change, to grow, to be confused. It's okay to fight for something and to want to give up. It's okay to want someone. It's okay to need someone. It's okay to learn and to get better and to know you're still not quite there yet. It's okay to suck at drawing hands. It's okay to be nervous and excited at the same time, to be unsure of what's ahead. It's okay to just go and try and to feel whatever you have to feel and to follow your gut. It's okay, because that's all you really have.

This went exactly how it needed to. I guess it usually does. Love revealed how covered up I was, but heartache broke me open.

I made it to Los Angeles, and it is going to be okay.